Live Your Humanity

Ron Hammond

Live Your Humanity

Activate Your
Innate Human Values
for a Meaningful
& Connected Life

NEW YORK

LONDON • NASHVILLE • MELBOURNE • VANCOUVER

Live Your Humanity

Activate Your Innate Human Values for a Meaningful and Connected Life

Published in New York, New York, by Morgan James Publishing. Morgan James is a trademark of Morgan James, LLC. www.MorganJamesPublishing.com

A **FREE** ebook edition is available for you or a friend with the purchase of this print book.

CLEARLY SIGN YOUR NAME ABOVE

Instructions to claim your free ebook edition:
1. Visit MorganJamesBOGO.com
2. Sign your name CLEARLY in the space above
3. Complete the form and submit a photo of this entire page
4. You or your friend can download the ebook to your preferred device

ISBN 9781631955709 paperback
ISBN 9781631955716 ebook
Library of Congress Control Number: 2021935170

Cover & Interior Design by:
Christopher Kirk
www.GFSstudio.com

Morgan James is a proud partner of Habitat for Humanity Peninsula and Greater Williamsburg. Partners in building since 2006.

Get involved today! Visit
MorganJamesPublishing.com/giving-back

Table of Contents

Introduction

nspiration often arrives spontaneously, and the inspiration to write this book was no exception. I experienced a common traffic event that most of us have experienced at one time or another. I was out one morning running a few errands, and as I was driving down a heavily populated three lane road in my city, I was cut off by another driver. Thankfully, I was able to avoid an accident by slamming the brakes and was also thankful that no other cars were involved. I'll admit that at first, I reacted in a predictable way, shouting a few expletives, but I quickly pulled myself together, cooled off and kept going on my way. Even though that event was relatively minor, it sparked a thoughtful reflection on just how human beings interact with one another today.

Over the last decade I've noticed that the pace of life has been steadily increasing. Our workplaces treat us as expendable assets and demand that we make ourselves available to them at all hours. The list of required daily tasks that must be accomplished continues to grow longer, and the pressure of time slipping away makes us stressed and anxious. These challenges shift our perspective away from thinking about others, creating distance between ourselves and the rest of the world. I believe this distance causes us to lose touch with the basic human values that all of us share, the core beliefs that help us develop meaning and connection in our lives. Integrity, kindness, compassion and love go dormant when we cease to cultivate and nurture them. Instead, we live our lives sitting in judgement, being fearful and ultimately giving up our peace.

For a long time, I experienced the negative effects of not living in my own human values. I was working in the information technology sector, going through a prolonged period of stress and anxiety that lasted for many years. My workdays were long, and I was managing a large team, juggling multiple projects that absorbed a tremendous amount of my mental capacity. I became run down, tired, and agitated, unable to focus on anything beyond what was in my own personal orbit. I lost the ability to express gratitude, to offer a simple kindness to others, and to offer love to those that were in my life. I let my human values go dormant. I felt like life had no meaning, leaving me disconnected from the rest of the world. This feeling set in so slowly that I didn't even realize that it was happening.

In this book, I'm going to show you how I empowered myself to change the direction of my life and to give myself a renewed sense of connection and meaning. I began by taking small steps, focusing first on love and gratitude while taking care to express to others just how much they meant to me. The results were fantastic, which provided the inspiration to continue to activate other values and continue to improve my life and outlook. Through sharing what I've learned, I hope that I can teach you how to have a similar awakening.

The chapters in this book will explore each one of the innate human values that will help you find this same meaning and connection for yourself. Each chapter will detail what a certain value means and offer an example(s) of how activating it can have positive effects for you. At the end of each chapter, I will offer you suggestions that you can use to help permanently activate each value for yourself. The book will also detail times where I was faced with life events that provided gentle reminders of how I should be living in my own activated human values. As you progress through the book, you will begin to discern how each one of the values are complementary to one another.

Activating these values is simple because they are already available to you and are easy to access. They only require a willingness to be aware of them and to consciously take steps to bring them into your own life. As you begin to awaken these values for yourself, you will discover that you are living an empowered life filled with satisfaction and contentment. You will also begin to notice that states of unease and anxiety will ease, freeing you to feel full of positivity and love. The benefits of living a life in this manner are enormous not only for you, but for the world, making it a much more tolerant, kind and loving place to live.

Thank you for reading and for being open to taking this journey with me.

CHAPTER 1

Activate Compassion and End Suffering

I've always been fascinated by what makes people tick. I'm keenly aware of almost every detail that they present to the world. I notice things like how they walk and their mannerisms, but my attention typically gravitates most strongly towards how they treat their fellow humans. There are times when our interactions with one another are not positive and kind and sometimes it feels like we don't understand what having compassion for one another really means. I've struggled with this myself in the past, but I recently had an experience that helped put me on the path to understanding what compassion really is.

How an alley and a bottle of water helped me understand suffering and develop compassion

The city that I currently live in is experiencing a homelessness crisis. The population of homeless people is rising and, as the available supply of housing becomes stretched and housing costs continue to climb, more and more people are in the unfortunate position of living on the street. For many years, encampments that house homeless people have existed downtown, but as the city has become more gentrified and growth has boomed, the homeless are looked upon as an unsavory aspect of the new, modernized landscape. Business owners and residents want them removed, and the city government has been exploring different measures to address the issue. Some of the measures developed, while made with the best of intentions, have instead resulted in harsh realities.

Approximately two years ago, in an attempt to move the homeless from the encampments, the police raided the camps and proceeded to block those areas of the city off so that they were no longer accessible. Unfortunately, while the homeless shelters perform an important role, there was (and still is) a lack of enough shelter space to accommodate everyone, forcing many to spread out miles away from the city center. Some of the encampments where they are now living are close to my neighborhood, and as I've driven or walked past them, I've noticed that a good many of them are densely populated. I've quietly wondered about what it must be like to live practically stacked on top of one another in confined, noisy and chaotic environments. But even as I understood that the situation wasn't ideal, I continued on with my day and never gave it a second thought. That was about to change.

One Monday, I walked into the alley behind my home to collect the emptied garbage bin and bring it into my backyard for storage. I was startled to see a homeless man sitting next to my garage. He was looking at me warily and when I acknowledged him, he said that he would be on his way shortly, that he was sitting next to my garage because he needed a quiet place to eat his lunch. I told him that he was just fine where he was and was welcome to hang out for a while. As I continued to pull the garbage bin into the backyard, it suddenly hit me that this man, who I would normally pass on the street without a word uttered between us, craved something that I take for granted every day. He simply wanted to eat his lunch in peace, away from the noise and chaos of his normal environment. I felt overcome by how hard his life must be and I had a strong desire to do something to help him.

I went inside my house and grabbed a bottle of water and took it to him, telling him that I noticed that he didn't have anything to drink with his lunch. Based on his reaction, you would have thought that I had given him the world. He was so grateful for such a small gesture, and it opened the door for the two of us to talk. I eventually asked him how he ended up in his situation. He told me that he was 35 years old and college educated, but that he had made some bad decisions that led to him living on the streets. He didn't elaborate on what those decisions were and I didn't ask, but he went on to explain that he was living in an encampment nearby. He said he preferred being there to being in a shelter because of the drug use and crime that runs rampant in those facilities. He explained that the likelihood of being assaulted in a shelter is quite high and that any possessions that you may have are frequently stolen if they're not watched closely. He said that he feels safer in the encampments or sleeping in an alley. After 15 more minutes of talking, we parted ways. Before I left, I told him that he was welcome to have his lunch next to my garage when he felt like he needed some peace and quiet.

That experience left a mark and defined for me what the true meaning of compassion is. When you feel bad for someone else's hardship and then help alleviate them of the suffering that comes from that hardship, you are living with compassion.

While our paths haven't crossed since that day, I frequently find my thoughts returning to him, wondering if he's doing OK. The empathy that I felt toward this gentleman helped me to understand his humanity, and it also helped me to feel and understand his emotions around his situation. Even though offering a tiny amount of help didn't solve all of his problems, at least I could do something.

I now look at everyone that I see each day a little differently, reminding myself that nothing is ever as it appears on the outside and that I don't have a clue what kind of challenges others face in their lives. I am filled with the desire to help others and am joyful at the prospect of doing so whenever I can.

What is compassion?

The Dalai Lama is the unifying symbol of the Tibetan state and is revered around the world as the human picture of compassion. If you've ever spent time reading his books or other writings, you have most likely noticed that compassion is a common element that drives his life. I recently came across a quote from him that perfectly sums up what he believes compassion to be: "I believe compassion to be one of the few things we can practice that will bring immediate and long-term happiness to our lives. I'm not talking about the short-term gratification of pleasures like sex, drugs or gambling (though I'm not knocking them), but something that will bring true and lasting happiness. The kind that sticks." To him, the more that we care about the happiness of other people, the greater our own sense of well-being becomes. When you have compassion for another person, you want to provide assistance in elevating someone from their suffering, which in turn makes you happy.

By now, you might be asking how you can offer compassion to other people, but there really isn't a one size fits all approach that fits each possible situation that you may find yourself in. The best thing that you can do is to increase your awareness of what is happening around you and be ready. Look for situations where you can be compassionate to someone and then offer it up. You'll feel good and so will they.

Why compassion matters

Why does compassion matter? The simple answer is that it makes life easier for others. Think about my interaction with the homeless man. While he chose (for understandable reasons) not to take advantage of the services of a homeless shelter, others do depend on shelters for an opportunity to sleep in a warm bed and eat a hot meal each day. Homeless shelters all over the country would have never been built if our communities didn't have at least some understanding of the suffering of the homeless. This is compassion. Also consider the compassion that you see in action after natural disasters, such as when a tornado rips through a town and destroys people's homes and businesses. Within hours, the citizens of that particular community come together to help their neighbors rebuild. It is compassion that drives their actions. You may also see compassion demonstrated after a large snowstorm, when neighbors gather together, snow shovels in hand, spending hours together shoveling sidewalks and digging cars out so that others can safely pass through.

I have actually heard people say that compassion is a weakness, but that is simply not true. Offering compassion is a sign of strength. I have witnessed people being moved to tears when they see compassion in action and this makes them view the person extending it in a favorable light. They're viewed as being trustworthy and humble, strong and dependable. So, the next time that you find yourself with an opportunity to extend compassion, put any thoughts of it casting you in a weak light out of your mind and offer it anyway. You'll be glad that you did.

Can you imagine what the world would be like right now if every governing body made compassion a cornerstone of their governing policy? There is a lot of division and lack of compassion in the world today. For example, the current crisis at the U.S. southern border is one of the most divisive in our history and there is a systemic lack of compassion for human beings that are attempting to flee circumstances that are unimaginable to most of us. Fear tactics are being used to create divisions that have fractured people into polarized groups on either side of the argument. The same thing is also occurring with the ongoing healthcare debate, where some elected officials are putting their own political interests ahead of their constituents, not making an effort to understand the negative impacts that a broken healthcare system is having on the average person. Some people are losing everything they have due to a healthcare insurance system that leaves them bankrupt when a major health event occurs.

These types of divisions are weakening the very foundation of society. It reminds me of Abraham Lincoln's quote "a house divided against itself cannot stand." Being brave and ginning up the willingness to remember that what affects one ultimately affects everyone provides a reminder that having compassion is a sign of strength.

If you want to see compassion in action, why it matters, and how it can become a major force in your life, spend some time volunteering in a local nonprofit that interests you. I have been fortunate to witness compassion first-hand while volunteering with the Ronald McDonald House in my city. For those of you who are unfamiliar with what the Ronald McDonald House is, it is like a hotel where families in need who have sick children can stay free of charge while their children receive medical care. It is heartwarming to witness the level of compassion that all of the staff freely share with the families that are staying there, and the families are so grateful for it. There are two house managers that I've worked with, Holly and Sandra, both of whom are walking examples of compassion. They get to know every single one of the families, what their children's illnesses are and how long their treatment will last. When a family needs anything, Holly and Sandra are right there to provide it to them. They listen to the struggles that these families face, and when the families are returning back to the house after a long day at the hospital, Holly and Sandra are there to greet them and offer an encouraging word. All of this comes from the heart, letting the residents know that they're cared for and supported. If you ever have an opportunity to volunteer or to financially support your local Ronald McDonald House, I encourage you to do so. I promise that seeing what compassion in action looks like will compel you to activate your compassion and share it with others.

You alone have the power to activate compassion within yourself and you also have the capacity to offer it at a moment's notice. It is the right thing for you to do, not only for your own benefit, but for the benefit of all of society. When you inevitably find yourself in a spot where you may not be comfortable extending compassion outwardly, quietly remind yourself that you already have it inside of you, notice how empowered you feel and then go for it. The rewards that you and society reap from doing so are immeasurable.

Identifying suffering in others

The key to offering compassion is to be able to identify when someone else is suffering. You may believe that suffering is the result of a painful physical event, such as when you break an arm or are healing from injuries due to an accident. While those experiences are indeed painful, they don't necessarily cause you to suffer. Suffering is caused by how you think about and resist what is occurring in your life at any given time. You may experience suffering when you suddenly find yourself without a job and are feeling lost and without a purpose, when you are dealing with an important decision and you don't know which way to turn, when you are in conflict with someone else because of something they either did or said that offended or hurt you or when you find yourself in a loop of negative emotional thoughts surrounding the ending of a relationship.

How someone experiences suffering is very unique and personal to them, so identifying it can be challenging. But if you're open and you have a little curiosity, you can quickly gain an understanding of what is triggering suffering in someone else. How do you do it? The simplest thing that when you notice someone is a little off, you can simply ask them what's going on. Merely asking can be so powerful. It says that you are there, that you care and that you are being sincere and are open to helping, which develops trust and makes it easier for someone to share with you what they're going through. It also helps to make an effort to spend time with someone who you know is going through a tough spot in their life. Make the time to share a meal or to sit down and really talk with them and you will provide a gateway for them to trust you. Eventually, they'll share what is causing them to suffer with you and also let you help them. The more often you do this, the easier it becomes, and you become a living and breathing example of compassion for others to follow.

Why compassion fatigue is detrimental

Life can sometimes become so busy that compassion takes a back seat. Your job demands more and more of you, leaving you feeling tired and worn out at the end of the day, and when you get home, your work begins again. Dinner has to be made, homework done, the clutter picked up and the children put to bed so that you can turn around and do it all over again the next day. Social media and the news inundate you with negative messages and it becomes overwhelming to process everything that is coming at you from all directions. This closes down the well of compassion that you have inside of you. This state of mind is called "compassion fatigue."

I believe that compassion fatigue has three components. The first component is the overwhelming amount of negative information that you receive every day surrounding happenings in your local community and all over the world. It's impossible for one person to process the astounding level of suffering that is occurring every day. As you first learn of these things, you probably feel a bit of concern around what's occurring, but then in an act of self-preservation, you quickly push it out of your mind telling yourself there's nothing that you can do to help the situation. It's natural for you to act in this way, but over time, as you are exposed to more information like this, you begin to instantly push it out of your mind without even thinking about it, closing off compassion.

Compassion fatigue can also make you dig in on your long-held beliefs. When you become blind to the suffering that's going on around you, you can find yourself believing that there is only one way to see the world. You may believe that someone is causing their own suffering through their actions. Do everything you can to cast your judgments aside and stop allowing your ego to take control of your thoughts. When you put your ego in charge, you shut down your ability to understand what is causing someone else's pain and suffering, making it virtually impossible to have feelings of compassion.

Finally, compassion fatigue is also caused by a lack of self-compassion. You cannot have real compassion for someone else unless you already have it for yourself. Be conscious of your inner dialogue telling you that you're not enough. These same thoughts tell you that you have to be perfect at every single thing that you do—and in turn you expect this kind of perfection from others, which can get in the way of compassion. You're human and you are not perfect by any stretch of the imagination. You will make mistakes, but these same mistakes help you to learn and contribute positively to your growth. Stop ruminating on what others may or may not think of you because in reality, they really aren't thinking about you all that much. They have their own issues, inner dialogues and mistakes that they're dealing with. Elevate yourself above the negative messages that you tell yourself and accept yourself for who you are right now.

The problems of the world are too big for anyone to handle individually, but you can have a positive impact on the spread of compassion by offering it up each day to those that are in your community or workplace. Remember, it doesn't have to be elaborate and grandiose, because sometimes the smallest acts of compassion have the largest impact. Sharing compassion is contagious and you have the power to make a positive and sustained impact on the world by taking the lead and allowing others to witness your acts of compassion.

How activated compassion benefits you

The phrase "it's better to give than to receive" is a perfect reflection of compassion. When you reflect back on times in your life when you have given something to someone else, whether it was a gift, your time or help, the feeling that most likely comes to your mind is a pronounced sense of pleasure. The same feelings come to you when you give compassion. Extending compassion to others improves your sense of well-being and it has its own built-in reward system that makes you want to do it over and over again.

When you activate compassion within yourself, you are consciously choosing to provide meaning to your life through the act of serving others. Compassion makes you feel purposeful and good about yourself, so it's natural that once you offer it to other people, you want to keep on doing so. You will also notice that you are not as stressed out and that you have lower levels of anxiety. Studies have proven that lower levels of stress lead to lower inflammation levels within the body, bringing with it the possibility of increased longevity.

Compassion also broadens your horizons and changes your perspective on long held beliefs that you may be holding in your mind. When you step out of your comfort zone, going deep within yourself to observe and think about what is causing someone else's suffering, you begin to have a new understanding of the world that you may have never considered before. You will find yourself softening on some of your beliefs and will experience an increased willingness to learn a different perspective on something that you may not have been comfortable with before.

Be conscious about noticing how you feel when you exercise compassion, and take note of the positive internal reactions to your new thought process. I'm sure that you will feel a sense of serenity and calm wash over you along with an unselfish willingness to help someone else end their suffering

Suggestions for activating compassion within yourself

- *In order to extend compassion to others, you must first have compassion for yourself.*
- *Remind yourself constantly that no matter what happens or what anyone believes or says about you, you are per-*

fect just the way you are at this very moment. Give your-self the space to appreciate and accept who and what you are, with all of your flaws and imperfections.

- *Increase your awareness of your immediate surroundings and your community so that you are proactively looking for ways to assist others. Take direct action by making a conscious effort to hold the door open for someone, to practice random acts of kindness towards other people without the expectation of receiving anything in return and to support organizations that help those who are in need by volunteering your time.*

- *When engaged in conversation, put forth the effort to employ your active listening skills by focusing on what someone is sharing with you. This takes a lot more effort than it does to talk about yourself, but when you do, you will receive hints about the pain that they're dealing with at that time and then have a chance to help them work through it. They'll feel heard and you will feel good because you have helped them.*

- *Make an effort to offer an encouraging word to those that you come in contact with each day. We are surrounded by negative messages all of the time and one message that is particularly harmful is when others believe that they don't measure up because of what has been said to them or about them. Try not to focus on things that you believe people do wrong and instead focus on what they're doing right. Then, don't be afraid to share that with them.*

- *Make a habit of always living in gratitude. This will be discussed more later in the book, but for now, remember to never underestimate the power of saying thank you. When you do this, you are telling the other person that you appreciate their efforts to help you and this is a great way to keep compassion activated. Say thank you to your hair stylist, and to the person who rings up your groceries at the supermarket. Offer a nice hand gesture as an acknowledgement to someone who lets you merge into the lane in front of them while driving. Your efforts will not go unnoticed and it just might activate the same mindset in them.*

Activating compassion in your life takes time and a little mental elbow grease, but the rewards are worth the effort. I'm reminded of an observation from Plato, the Greek Philosopher, that perfectly sums up his thoughts on compassion: "Be kind, for everyone you meet is fighting a harder battle." I think this is pretty good advice to live by! Make a conscious effort to practice the steps offered above to activate compassion within you and see for yourself how doing so positively influences your ability to live your humanity.

CHAPTER 2

Activate Love and Eradicate Separation

"Love Makes the World Go 'Round" is a famous song by soul singer Deon Jackson, and the lyrics to this song were the inspiration for this chapter. The lyrics of the song mention that love is the reason that trees and flowers grow, that the birds sing and also that people come together. I can't think of a better way to describe the real meaning of love.

Love is the reason that we are here. It's the glue that binds us together and helps us to support and care for one another. Love is in everything, but it feels like we're losing sight of this today. The hustle of life and constant obligations, stress at the office and the vitriol that we're seeing in politics are all dividing and separating us. The rise of social media has people focused on their electronic devices and not on each other and we're drifting apart, leaving love on the sidelines.

I struggled to define what love meant for most of my life, and it took some deep introspection in my adult years to eventually figure out how to turn my thoughts away from these modern-day challenges and redirect them towards love. While your life and challenges are most certainly different from mine, the end result is still the same. Right now, you may be experiencing the very same feelings of separation and struggle with love that I did, but there is a way to solve the issue that provides a lasting positive impact and brings love permanently into your thoughts.

How I learned the importance of love

When I was five years old, my parents divorced. It was the end of a very tumultuous marriage. While I do believe that they tried their best to make their marriage work, it's very clear to me now that they really were not meant to be together. Over time, I witnessed arguments over the most mundane things and I felt the hurt feelings that both of them experienced. This made me retreat into my own world as a way of soothing myself. I became very withdrawn. This continued on for a couple of years until the arguing became unsustainable. I clearly remember the day that my parents were having a calm and serious discussion about what they were going to do going forward. I very quietly walked out of my room and went down the hall to the edge of the living room, where I saw my mother sitting in her rocking chair and my father sitting on the couch, having a very tense discussion. I remember feeling that the end was coming near, which of course upset me very much and made me feel like my whole world was crumbling. The anchor of my family was cut free and sinking, leaving me feeling vulnerable.

The divorce came, and as time passed, both of my parents eventually found other spouses and remarried. This was a huge adjustment for all of us, but I especially struggled and my withdrawal became even more pronounced. Overnight, I gained a stepfather who had never had a son before, and it was difficult for him to be a father to a son that he hardly knew. We had a very complicated relationship with one another that turned negative many times. I also had a very complicated relationship with my natural father, and both of these situations left me feeling alone in the world. Eventually, as time carried on, both relationships disintegrated to the point of uncomfortable tolerance and I continued to shrink down and retreat into the background.

As I became an adult, I had a very low opinion of myself and I never felt as if I fit in or was truly accepted. I transferred my insecurities to other people in the form of internal criticisms and petty jealousies. I convinced myself that their lives were much better than mine and that I was a mess compared to them. I struggled with friendships and making connections with others. I didn't take the time to really learn about people and just love them for what and who they were. My external interactions were always pleasant, but my negative thoughts were destroying my ability to truly connect with and love others. This was very painful and I knew that I had to do something.

The ticket out of my conundrum came to me in my early thirties. I was doing some work in the yard when, out of the blue, I suddenly began reflecting back on a conversation that I had one summer day with my great grandmother. I had never given this conversation much thought before, but I believe that there must have been some divine guidance that brought it to my mind so clearly that it felt like it was happening in real time.

When I was young and unable to stay at home alone, I frequently spent my summer breaks with my great grandparents. To me, they were the picture of patience and wisdom and the love that they showered on their family was overwhelming. My great grandmother was especially strong in her faith and had a large, outgoing presence that radiated love in all directions. She was active in her church and community and she volunteered in numerous organizations that helped others that were in need. Her arms were open to everyone and she greeted everyone with a hug and a giant smile. She was a magnet of love and anyone who arrived anywhere near her orbit couldn't help but to be drawn to her. She never had a negative or harsh word about anyone.

One day, I was in the car with her, and I was having a particularly tough day. I was feeling lonely and a little unloved and really questioning why I even existed. I filled her in on what was going on and then I asked her why she believed we are here. Without skipping a beat, she told me that we're here because we're loved. She said that love sustains, nurtures and protects us as we move through our life and that it's our obligation to keep that love moving by freely sharing it with other people and without conditions. Her view was that a lot of the problems in the world could be solved if people simply believed in their hearts that they were loved. She believed that the world would see an end to fear and strife by embracing love. This sounds pretty simple today, but my 9-year-old brain had a difficult time wrapping my mind around it.

She continued to explain to me that each one of us is unique and that we came into this life to bring our specific gifts to the world and to learn lessons that are beneficial to our individual soul's growth. Paramount to those lessons is learning how to love and accept others for who they are, no matter what. While we're learning those lessons, we must remember that each of us is a human example of God's love for us and that it's our obligation to use that love for the greater good of the world and to act in support of and in service to others.

I find myself reflecting back on that conversation often, and it always reminds me of what the real definition of love is: being a beacon of love means dedicating yourself to being of service to other people. Living that way today has brought tremendous joy, and makes life feel free and fulfilling. I still have the same worries that I've always had, but they no longer weigh on my mind or cause worry like they once did because I know that a solution with love as its basis is already on its way. I know that when I'm challenged with a situation where I may not have all of the answers, that the right person with the right information will show up on time to help me solve any dilemma. It also helps me to offer love to myself, which squelches my ego and stops the counterproductive and negative mind chatter. This opens the channel to my trusted intuition and provides confidence that I can move through life's challenges with ease and confidence.

My great grandmother lived to be 100 years old and I'm convinced that was because she used the love that was inside of her to be of service to others. She was a living and breathing example to everyone of what activated love looks like and my family is better for having had her.

Know in your heart that no matter what is occurring in your life, you are loved. Amplify that same love through acts of service to others and then notice how your thoughts and your life change in a loving and positive way, knocking down any barriers to happiness and fulfillment.

Common barriers to activating and sharing love

Your ego is powerful, and it controls how you respond to external events. It has the power to send negative messages that can make you act in a way that deactivates the love inside of you. Your interactions with family, friends and coworkers as well as the images that you observe on social media, television and online advertisements, unconsciously tell you that if you really want to be loved, you have to look or act in a certain way or belong to the right social circle. Your ego eats this right up. This is an illusion, but nevertheless, your ego's buy-in can make you believe that you're less than or separate from others. Though that simply isn't true, its power is undeniable. Before you're even aware of it, your negative view of yourself can make you unconsciously erect barriers to sharing your love. Some of the most common barriers are discussed below:

Lack of self-love

Just as we discussed in the last chapter with the importance of self-compassion, in my experience, lack of self-love is the most damaging barrier that you can erect. While it may sound a bit cliché, loving and being kind to yourself is absolutely the most important thing that you can do to bring the innate love that is inside of you into the world. Self-love comes from within. When you don't have it, you look outside of yourself for approval, which means you give all of your power away to the opinions of other people. Other people— who may not even know you and who you will most likely never meet begin to control how you feel about your life. Unless you consciously stop others from influencing you, you find yourself in an endless cycle of comparison and striving, always looking for external goals to use as a measure of your worthiness. Believe me, it will never be enough, because even if you do manage to acquire all of the things that make your life seem better at a given moment, that feeling will only last a short while before you go in search of the next bigger and better thing. Stop worrying about driving the most current car, owning the latest items in fashion or going to the trendiest restaurants. It's fine if you enjoy doing those things, but do them because you want to, not because you feel like you have to.

If you don't believe anything else that you read in this book, please believe this: you are enough just the way you are. You are already perfect in the eyes of your creator. You are loved unconditionally, so do all that you can to adopt this same mindset towards yourself. You don't need material things in order to be loved; you don't need to live in an affluent neighborhood or to be envied by others. When you find yourself thinking about your perceived shortcomings and are tempted to look for perfection outside of yourself, please remind yourself of this. With patience and practice, you will love and respect yourself and that will open the door for you to share your love with others.

Practicing self-love is easy and it comes down to just a few things that you can do every day. First and foremost, check your ego and make a conscious effort to calm that inner voice that tells you that you're not enough. Be mindful to put a stop to any thoughts that make you measure yourself against other people and also tell you that you're not enough. Other peoples' opinions of you are just opinions. They simply do not matter! If you find your inner voice delivering negative messages to you about your intelligence, material possessions, or the way you live your life, focus immediately on something positive about yourself by reflecting on successful past accomplishments that you've enjoyed and have gratitude for all that is already in your life (more on gratitude in the next chapter). You will feel that burden immediately lift. Put an end to striving for perfection and give yourself a break. You are not going to achieve perfection with everything in your life and setting your sights on perfection creates an unnecessary amount of stress and brings your negative inner voice forward to belittle and mock you. Finally, do everything that you can to curtail complaining. When you complain, you live in a state of resistance to reality, which can potentially mean you miss out on a gift or a divine lesson that particular moment holds for you. Complaining takes away your energy and it gives all of your power to the thoughts that you're dissatisfied with, shifting your focus away from connecting with and loving yourself.

Casting Judgment

Another powerful barrier to love is judgment. Casting your judgment on others is one of the most damaging things that you can do. Judgments are natural; your life experiences helped your thoughts begin to grow and mature and you developed judgments to help guide you successfully along your life's path. But these very judgments that have served you well in most cases and helped you successfully navigate challenges have a tendency to take root in your mind. When they do this, they become a barrier to love. Your ego believes that it's always right no matter what, and it becomes adept at figuring out ways to turn your judgments in a negative direction, closing you to different points of view. When this happens, you develop unfavorable thoughts about other people based on their religion, skin color, social status, income level, sexual orientation or intelligence, for example. These types of judgments make you believe that you are superior to others—but in reality, this is just your ego taking control of the wheel.

To combat this, raise your awareness by paying close attention to all of your thoughts and then making a mental note of any judgments that you notice. When you judge, you are seeing the world as you believe it is, not as it really is. And when you notice your judgments, they begin to release their control over you and how you view others.

Of course, this can be easier said than done. It takes effort on your part to become aware of what you're feeling and thinking when judgments creep into your thoughts. As you grow your awareness through continual monitoring of your thoughts, you must consciously make the effort to stop them in their tracks when they first appear. Awareness is kryptonite to ego-driven judgments, and by becoming aware of them and confronting them head on, you slowly chip away at your ego's ability to lord them over you. It's not easy at first and you will find yourself slipping, but when you do feel your ego taking over, immediately stop yourself and make a conscious decision to shift them in a positive direction.

Over time and with a lot of practice, I promise you that your revised way of thinking will become second nature. You will begin to see differences as a chance to learn something new and as an opportunity to bring your love forward and reconnect with everyone, positively living your humanity. When you cease judging and remind yourself that every single person on earth is walking their path the best way that they know how, you begin to know within yourself that the differences between us are a learning opportunity and a chance to bring everyone closer together and let love expand. Throw all of your judgments aside and accept everyone for who they are.

The low energy act of gossip

Every action that you take and each thought that you think has an impact on how you feel. Acting and thinking in positive ways and exploring pursuits that interest you are examples of positive habits that give you energy and make you feel good inside. Negative habits, such as carrying resentments and anger sap your energy and cause you to feel bad. Gossiping is one of those low energy habits that not only negatively impacts how you feel but also acts as a barrier to sharing your love with the world. Gossiping serves no other use than to feed your ego by telling you that you are superior to someone else. I had an experience with gossiping several years ago that taught me a lot about its negative effects which, and that experience still sticks with me today.

When I graduated from college, I began my career working for a large organization in the Washington, DC area. I remember being very eager and excited to begin this new chapter in my life and I had expectations of making new and exciting connections, earning a paycheck and truly being on my own, forging my unique path in life. My first day on the job was exciting. My new manager introduced me to my co-workers and gave me a tour of the building. I got down to business with my first job assignment, and as time progressed, I began to fit in and become accepted as a part of the team. We frequently ate lunch together, sharing humor and stories about our personal lives outside of the office. The team eventually became a part of my social network outside of work, too. We were cohesive and it seemed perfect and I was optimistic about my future there despite the huge learning curve that I was facing.

One day, a large group of us went to the building cafeteria to have lunch. One person at the table began to talk about one of our fellow co-workers in an unfavorable way. The woman that they were talking about had become a friend of mine and I remember feeling conflicted. We wouldn't have said some of the things that were said had she been sitting at the table with us and I was very angry with myself for not standing up to stop the conversation. But eventually, groupthink began to take over and everyone became involved in the conversation, including me. Some of the comments were quite hurtful: she wore weird clothes, her hair was oily and the cut was outdated, it was really unprofessional that she didn't wear makeup. I knew it was wrong to talk about her this way, but I willingly participated because I wanted to be accepted with the group.

As the conversation continued, we didn't notice that the object of our gossip was sitting at the table next to us with a different group of people. We only realized that she was there when she got up from the table to make her way back upstairs to her desk. Everyone at our table instantly became quiet and there were a lot of red faces, including my own. I felt terrible and my stomach was twisted up like a knot at how we had just treated this wonderful woman. She confronted me as I was walking to the parking garage after work that evening, letting me know that she heard what we said about her. I apologized, but it didn't matter. The damage was done. Unfortunately, we never mended fences after that, and I will never forget that pained look on her face. Even now, 20 years later, I still experience the same knotting up of my stomach and guilty feelings about our actions that day.

When you engage in gossip, you are closing your love off to others in an effort to temporarily make yourself feel good. But while the high of gossiping may be short lived, its negative effects linger. Gossip takes the humanity out of the person that you're talking about. It makes you an energy drain not only to yourself but also to the person or people that you're gossiping with, lowering their ability to also share their love with the world. You simply don't look good in the eyes of others, even if they are outwardly agreeing with you.

Whenever are about to engage in gossip about someone, take notice of how you're feeling, because most likely, you're experiencing negative feelings inside of yourself. Those feelings are a gentle warning from your body to stop doing what you're doing. When you have the urge to gossip, resist that urge with everything that you have, and when you find yourself in a situation where gossiping is occurring around you, quietly excuse yourself from it and walk away. Take notice of how you're feeling at that moment. I bet that you will feel happier and lighter and when you feel this way, you are removing the barriers to separation and are better able to contribute your part to making the world a much more loving and kinder place for everyone.

Lack of Gratitude

One last barrier to sharing your love with the world is in having a lack of gratitude. I'll dig a little deeper on this topic in a coming chapter, but for now, please believe this: you have much to be grateful for in your life. You woke up this morning, you have a roof over your head and you most likely have food to put on the table. You have a body that takes care of everything for you, fighting off disease, digesting your food and unconsciously controlling your breathing, carrying oxygen into your cells so that your heart can continue to beat and your brain continue to function. When you consciously remember that everything is here to support you and that all that you see around you is here specifically for your best interest, it elevates your gratitude.

By having gratitude, you stop separating yourself from everything and everyone, and you begin to see the world in a new and positive light. After some time, practicing gratitude begins to become second nature, requiring little to no effort on your part. You will find yourself becoming appreciative and thankful for everything that comes into your life, to include both the good and the bad and you begin to see everything bathed in the light of love. You view the world as a kinder place which helps you share your kindness with other people, opening the door to reconnecting with humanity.

What someone who has activated love looks like

You have the power to make a significant change on the world by freely sharing the abundant love that is already inside of you with others. There is probably already someone in your life today that is an example of this for you to follow and you may not even realize it. People like this are out there and you can easily find them if you take the time to become aware.

The type of person that I'm talking about is someone who lights up a room when they walk into it, not necessarily because they are extroverted, but because others can sense their deep levels of inner peace and joy. They aren't just nice to everyone, rather, they're *kind* to everyone. Being nice is treating people well and acting politely toward them, while being kind comes from the heart and is transmitted through caring and loving acts toward other people.

People that share their love are also enthusiastic and approach everything that they do with a "can-do" attitude. They look at acts of service for others as something that they get to do rather than as something that they have to do. They know that when they are finished, they have accomplished something that contributes to the greater good of everyone. They share their knowledge openly and willingly and are always ready to lend a helping hand whenever they can. They also spend time in their community, volunteering for organizations that support those that are less fortunate than them and they do it with a smile on their face and with joy in their heart.

People that share their love also have no preconceived ideas about people. They don't judge anyone, accepting others for who they are with no inherent bias in their minds about how someone should or should not be. They go the extra mile to welcome everyone by inviting them into their lives with a smile and open arms. They're also friendly and approachable and, while they may have a lot of friends, they spend their time with a few select close friends that share their same loving values and outlook on life. They already know the incalculable value of being around people who share their same view of the world and fill their emotional energy bank by communing with them, which in turn energizes them to continue sharing their love.

People who share their love are also cognizant of their limitations. They put their ego aside and ask for help when they need it. They accept constructive criticism and seek out those people that have more knowledge than they do on a particular subject. They learn everything that they can so that they can help when someone comes to them seeking that same knowledge.

People who share their love with the world admit and learn from their mistakes. They say that they are sorry when they've hurt someone and then they remember what happened so that they can do better next time.

And, finally, people that share their love smile and they smile often. They have large, beaming, radiant smiles that make others feel good, safe and accepted.

Five suggestions for activating the love that is already inside of you

- *Forget about the opinions of other people. When you focus on what other people think of you, you give all of your power away to them and this shuts down the flow of love. Cultivate activities that you can participate in to elevate the view that you hold of yourself by adopting a new exercise routine, exploring new cooking techniques or by taking on a new hobby, for example. When you focus on and love yourself in a healthy way, you no longer need or desire the opinions of other people, freeing you up to share your love.*

- *Pay careful attention to your judgments of others. Invite healthy and positive conversations with those whose opinions differ from your own and walk away from any situation that may entice you into the low energy act of gossiping. You'll feel much better for doing so.*

- *Actively be on the lookout for opportunities to be of service to others as you go about your daily routine. Offer assistance or a kind word without any expectation of receiving anything in return. When you do this, notice the activation of good feelings inside of you and use those feelings as a springboard to make you want to continue being of service.*

- *Express delight in others' successes. Put an end to the petty jealousies that crop up when you start comparing your life to theirs. When you take the time to become aware and put an internal premium on the positive things that you bring into every situation that you encounter in your life, you will begin to notice that any envy that you may feel will gradually evolve into strong and loving relationships.*

- *Smile often, taking notice of the feelings that you are experiencing inside of yourself when you do so. You'll most likely notice that other people will be uncomfortable with a random stranger smiling at them, but do it anyway. When you smile, it's almost impossible for you to remain closed and unapproachable. Smiling also makes you feel good, and when you feel good, you naturally want to share your love. You will find that people are naturally drawn to you and feel safe in your presence, which gives you more opportunities to establish connection and find meaning in those connections.*

These suggestions are the very same steps that I followed, but you may have other steps that you choose to follow. There is no one size fits all approach to love. Always think about how love can be a positive influence in your life and then notice how it pays great dividends to your emotional well-being when activated. When you concentrate on activating love in your life, you will first notice the development of loving and supportive thoughts that then naturally turn into loving and supportive actions toward other people which ultimately provides meaning and connection.

CHAPTER 3

Activate Gratitude and Experience Fulfillment

I n the last chapter, we discussed the dangers of basing your happiness and fulfillment on material things you own or how others may perceive you. Our materialistic society champions the accumulation of possessions and steadily climbing the career ladder as a way to make you believe that your life is complete, but I argue that those things aren't nearly as important as exercising gratitude for everything that is already in your life at this moment.

When I first tried to consciously feel gratitude, I found it challenging. It took a focused effort on my part to keep making progress with my gratitude, but those efforts finally paid off. I discovered that I was seeking fulfillment in things that were outside of myself. My thoughts would constantly drift toward how happiness would arrive with certain milestones, such as getting that promotion that I really wanted, or when I was able to acquire material things like the shiny and fast European sports sedan that I had my eye on for a long time. I was neck deep in the illusion that my fulfillment and happiness would come from achieving and acquiring. You may discover that you're being held back by the same kind of thinking. As we've already discussed, this kind of thinking is a circular trap, because once you achieve more or acquire more, you will experience an initial positive bump in your level of fulfillment, but you inevitably begin to set your focus on the next thing to acquire or milestone to achieve. I believe that there really is an easier and more effective way to feel fulfilled. One that has lasting staying power and which opens your eyes to all of the goodness that already surrounds you. You get this by adopting gratitude as a guiding principle in your life.

What is Gratitude?

The short definition of gratitude is being thankful for all that you have. I believe that the real power of gratitude lies in the positive feelings that you experience when you are truly grateful. By focusing on the positive feelings that arise inside of you each time that you're reflecting on what you're grateful for, you are experiencing gratitude first-hand. Gratitude comes from within, and while you can express your thanks externally, it means nothing if you don't feel that thanks on the inside.

I remember a few times in the past where I received a gift that I wasn't all that crazy about. I'm sure that you have experienced those same type of moments in your life, too. Since it's polite to express thanks even though you may not have been thankful, you probably said thanks anyway in order to avoid causing embarrassment or anger to the person who gave the gift to you. That's not gratitude. With true gratitude, you're actually physically experiencing the feeling of thankfulness on the inside. This is why it's such a powerful tool for expanding your fulfillment.

Why Gratitude matters

Believe me when I say that practicing gratitude really matters because of the positive changes that occur inside of you when you do so. As you practice, you will notice that your feelings of gratitude expand and make you happier, which has a positive effect on your physical and mental health. You will begin to notice that your inner thoughts begin to move away from the negative, freeing your mind from spending unproductive time churning on those thoughts. You will notice marked changes in your level of fulfillment, which has a positive effect on how you develop connections with other people.

When I adopted practicing gratitude for myself, I noticed those positive changes. Even better, all of the negative emotions around my personal challenges completely exited my mind. They simply ceased to be a factor in my life. Since I developed my practice five years ago, I really haven't had one bad day since. Sure, I have had days that have their challenges and roadblocks just like everyone else does, but they don't derail me. Life continues to move in the right direction and I credit my practice of gratitude for that outcome.

How I was led to activate gratitude

A few years ago, I faced a career upheaval that turned my life upside down and shook me to the very core, leaving me feeling rudderless and out of control. I began my career 27 years ago working for a large Information Technology (IT) organization where I held various increasingly challenging roles in Corporate Finance. I learned a great deal, developed a vast support network within the company and worked with some very smart people. My efforts paid off because I was able to move into a senior level role, leading a large team of 37 people. My performance reviews were excellent and I consistently received praise from my leaders for a job well done. My paycheck was competitive and I was content. This continued for quite a long time, but as the market for IT services began to soften, the company ended up going through some rough times, which caused difficulties for all 150,000 of the employees working there. Contracts were lost, customers began to tighten their belts and revenues and profits began to plummet. Raises and bonuses evaporated, and things became so challenging financially that the company began counting every penny, even tracking the number of pens taken from the office supply closet. Times looked bleak, and eventually the company was acquired by another organization. They were supposed to be our savior, but it didn't turn out that way. The new company didn't have a clear picture of what to do with this well entrenched organization and the integration of the two companies was a years-long disaster. In an attempt to bring the combined organization to profitability, multiple procedural changes began to be implemented. Financial forecasts were revamped, sales quotas were revised upward, a new bench of customers with deep wallets were being sought and enhancements to staff training were executed. The intention was for the company to have best in class staff and less red tape to slow down progress, but in the end, the efforts missed their mark by a great distance. The financial losses kept piling up and eventually staff layoffs began.

Resentment began to build, and the culture became tense and very competitive. My workload increased substantially and I was stressed beyond my capacity to handle it. I was working 12-hour days with no breaks while trying to keep my team satisfied and motivated. My workload was out of control.

After seven years of working in this environment, I realized that I needed to do something to get my sanity back, so I resigned. This was a difficult decision, as my co-workers were like my family and I had developed good relationships with my direct reports, but I knew that if I wanted to stay healthy, I had to exit the company.

I accepted a role with a much smaller organization and was excited to begin a new position. Throughout the interview process, I was informed that they wanted some new thinking on the existing team. I had plans to bring what I had learned from my previous experience to the new organization. My first day was filled with meet and greets and getting to know the job, and while it initially looked great, within the first two days of starting my new position, the realization set in that I was working in a very negative environment. My leader had severe control issues and didn't trust anyone to complete their work without a lot of micromanagement, leading to endless wasted time as we pointlessly reworked the same ideas over and over. I felt uninspired and completely lost, wondering what taking this job had done to my career. How could this be that the past success that I enjoyed didn't parlay into my new role? I considered resigning after the first two weeks, but that felt like quitting, so I decided to continue on with hopes that the situation would change. Unfortunately, it didn't. It actually worsened to the point where my leader and I couldn't communicate with each other and could hardly stand to be in the same room together. After a year in the new role, I was abruptly let go with no warning and hardly an explanation. I was stunned.

At first, I was relieved, almost giddy, that this chapter in my life was over. I walked out of that building relieved and with my head held high, confident that everything was going to work out quickly. But as time marched on and my efforts to secure another job were met with silence, my thoughts began to change and darken. I discovered that it can be difficult to find a job when you're in your forties. Bitter resentments and fear took over my reality and I found myself brooding for long stretches of time. It wasn't at all healthy and I eventually fell into a depression, which was made deeper by feeling like

I had no control over my life and that I had nowhere to turn.

After a fruitless months-long job search, I finally reached my breaking point. I found myself crying out in my mind that I needed help finding my next steps and that I needed it fast. I was pleading and begging for something to wrap my hands around and, unfortunately, what was returned to me was stony silence. Days and weeks passed with nothing, and I was beginning to feel like my efforts were a waste of time. My anger and sadness subsequently deepened and I was becoming even more disconnected from the outside world.

Then one day, a Tuesday morning to be exact, everything changed. I was mindlessly scrolling a social media app where I stumbled across an article on the benefits of gratitude. I began reading, and the deeper that I went into the article, the more I became completely enthralled with the message. I could hear my inner voice practically screaming at me from deep inside that this is what I needed to see at that moment. As I continued to read, I realized that I had been approaching my situation from the wrong angle. Over the next few days, my thoughts kept returning to this article and the more that I dwelled on those thoughts, the more I realized that all was not lost and I began to take steps to make gratitude a part of my daily thinking.

How Activating Gratitude Benefits You

If you want to experience feelings of sustained fulfill-ment, gratitude is the ticket. The concept of a gratitude practice sounds simple on the surface, but it's going to take a little work and heightened awareness on your part to make it happen. This is because your ego is most certainly going to get in the way of you being able to direct your thoughts towards gratitude. As you already know, the ego always thinks that it's right and it wants what it wants, so in order to get yourself to feeling fulfilled, you have to train your ego to step off to the side.

You can do this by first turning your focus towards all of the negative mind chatter that's going on. This is the same chatter that tells you that you're not good enough and makes you focus on your worries, your challenges and everything else that you perceive as being wrong in your life. You'll be surprised by how much negative chatter is actually going on in your mind when you take the time to really pay attention to it. It fills your head with bad thoughts, and before you know it, you're stuck in a negative loop, which makes you feel unhappy and unfulfilled.

If you want to stop these thoughts, you must first become fully aware of them. Then you must con-sciously put a stop to them by replacing them with good thoughts. Gradually, an attitude of gratitude can begin to take over. What you are doing is training your mind to focus on the positive and all of the good things that are already in your life. This will take some time and effort, so don't expect full results overnight, but keep at it. As you continue, you will notice a change in how you are feeling each time that you replace a negative thought with a positive thought, and this will give you the impetus to charge ahead and keep at it in order to make this change permanent. Take the time to go slowly and work your way up to a continual focused awareness of how you are feeling and what you are thinking. With time and patience, I promise you that you will begin to experience fulfillment in your life.

As you continue with your gratitude routine, you will begin to notice something very interesting occurring, which is that your mind will become more focused on the present. When I began to fully appreciate gratitude, I noticed that my thoughts became more oriented towards the present than the past or future, which made me feel good about my possibilities. It's really difficult to not have this feeling when you're present enough to notice all of the good that is already around you. For example, when I focus on the present and take a moment to appreciate the trees outside of my window, the beautiful Rocky Mountains off in the distance or the roof that is over my head, it's impossible not to well up with gratitude. You too will notice that more positive events begin to organically fall into place easily and with little effort on your part. This is how gratitude expands and makes your life fulfilling!

Gratitude makes you treat people better, which not only attracts people to you and boosts your social life, but also makes your existing friendships stronger. If you're the type of person that gets your energy from being around others, you will notice a marked increase in your energy levels. Humans need connections with others to thrive and to survive, and practicing gratitude makes it much easier for you to satisfy this basic need. Even if you don't get your energy from being around other people, it's still good because the interactions that you do have with others in your everyday life will also be positive and make both you and them feel good. It's a win-win no matter what.

Your health will also improve. There have been multiple studies on gratitude's positive health effects and they conclude that gratitude will enhance how you feel physically. People who regularly practice gratitude have reported having fewer aches and pains, increased energy levels and good sleep. I noticed that having gratitude gave me the desire to exercise more, which led me to take long walks every day with my dog, who didn't complain one bit about it. Give it a try and see if the same works for you.

Another positive effect of gratitude is that it makes you take the focus off of yourself. You become a lot less self-centered, which in turn ushers in positive interactions and lasting connections with other people. I'm sure that you've noticed how you feel inside and how emotionally and energetically draining it is to be around someone who is self-centered. Whenever you find yourself in a situation like this, take notice of how you're feeling at that moment and also notice the hit to your energy level. Then, focus on something to be grateful for and act as an observer to what is occurring in front of you. You will then see the lesson learned for you in a situation such as this and you'll walk away from it feeling great.

Five suggestions for activating gratitude in your life

- *Identify at least three things that you can be thankful for every day, and then journal about them. This is what sparked my gratitude and put it into turbo mode. Be sure to write about the positive feelings that these three things bring to you and how your life is better because of them. I use a gratitude app on my computer, but feel free to use whatever medium works for you. Doing this daily might take you 15 minutes and it gets you into the mindset of looking for all of the positive things that are already in your life.*

- *Write thank you notes. When someone has done something that makes you feel good or that you're especially appreciative of, tell them. People love to receive a personally written note and this goes a long way in activating your gratitude and making them view you in a positive light. It also helps to get you focused on the good that is already around you and makes the recipient of your appreciation want to continue to do the very thing that you're thanking them for, thus paying it forward for others.*

- *Take your thoughts back to how your life would be right now if something that you are especially grateful for didn't occur. This helps you appreciate how things from your past positively affect your now. I like to think back to my time in college and how having that experience helped develop lasting friendships and expanded the way that I think about the world. For you, it could be your home or your family. Whatever works is perfect.*

- *When you first wake up in the morning, before you've gotten out from under the covers, take a moment to say a silent thank you for having a brand new day ahead of you. As you go through your day, be thankful for your lunch, the colleague that is a little difficult to deal with and the car or public transportation that is taking you back home at the end of the day. Then, before you close your eyes to go to sleep, say another silent thank you for the day that you just had.*

- *Meditate on how grateful you are. This is effective because it helps to change your subconscious into a sustained way of grateful thinking. There are many free apps available that work well and will also help guide you through a successful meditation session. If you are new to meditating, it will be a little difficult to stop your mind from wandering at first, but keep on going with it and I promise that you will eventually see sustained positive results for yourself.*

At the beginning of this chapter, I suggested that you do not need material things to experience living a happy and fulfilled life. By now, I hope that you have effective tools in place that you can use and forever reference to make living a happy fulfilled life the norm for you. With a constant focus on gratitude, you will experience deeper and more meaningful connections that provide you with the life that you richly deserve. Keep your gratitude practice going and see how positively your life unfolds. You will no longer have to imagine fulfillment because it will become your norm.

CHAPTER 4

Activate Joy
and Be at Peace

What do you think about when you hear the word joy? When I asked myself this question for the first time, I thought joy and happiness were the same thing. Closer inspection of their meanings paints a difference picture of their definitions. Happiness is a feeling that you have when everything in your life seems to be going just as you want it to, but joy is an attitude that is unwavering, no matter what is going on in your life. You might experience happiness when you get that fancy new car that you've been eyeing, but over time that happiness begins to dissipate, especially when you get that first expensive repair bill. If you have an underlying attitude of joy as the baseline of everything that you do, that expensive repair bill won't have any effect whatsoever on the joy in your life.

As I was developing my thoughts for this chapter, I started first by taking some time to remember the people I've known that seemed to exude joy. I'm lucky that I have been surrounded by friends and family members who always seem to be filled with joy no matter what. One person that really sticks out in my mind the most is one of my uncles. Unfortunately, he passed while I was writing this chapter, but he had such a positive and joyful outlook on life that he was impervious to bad news or negative events that he faced. If he was ever met with a roadblock, he joyfully charged ahead and found a way around it, never letting his emotions get in the way of achieving his objective. He had an ebullient and warm personality, and was always wearing a smile on his face, living in a constant state of joy and peace no matter what was going on around him.

You too can live this way, because being joyful is your birthright. You are already preprogrammed to live a life that is filled with joy because you have an unlimited well of it already inside of you, but what has the potential to block your joy is the negative thinking that easily invades your present moments. Just as we discussed in the last chapter on gratitude, your thinking has an effect on how you feel, and if you observe your thoughts, you'll most likely notice that they almost always center on what you think is missing from your life. Negative thoughts—such as how someone may have mistreated you in the past, or worries about not having enough money or the nicest home, for instance—will always suppress your joy. You may also be living fearfully, unable to trust the power that is already inside of you that helps you to make good decisions and to move forward in your life. You may even experience trouble believing in your abilities to tackle any obstacle that may come your way. These types of thoughts can bring you to a lower energy feeling, which ultimately takes away your joy and your peace. It's perfectly normal to experience this, but it doesn't have to be a permanent fixture in your mind. You can turn your thoughts around by putting an end to the blocks to joy that you are experiencing. When you end this resistance, you begin to develop a clear picture of just how perfect everything about you and your life already is and how abundant you already are, ushering in a path to joy and peace. This chapter is going to help you get there.

How your thoughts take your joy away

When you begin to realize that you may not be experiencing as much joy as you want to, take a breath and step back. Make an effort to examine your thoughts and how they are potentially sabotaging your joy. We've already discussed how your thoughts affect you, and it's worth considering them again. Make an effort to check in with yourself to see how you're feeling as you move through your day. By doing this, you begin to see a pattern in your thinking that will help you understand just how your thoughts are blocking joy from being an influential part of your life. I did this for myself over a period of two months, and I'll share some of the thoughts that I was having. I bet that you will notice some of the same things with yourself.

The thinking that was most destructive to my joy was in comparing myself to others. Teddy Roosevelt once said that "comparison is the thief of joy" and I can say without a doubt that this is true. I was constantly comparing my home to their home, what I believed their bank accounts to be versus mine and judging myself on what kind of car I was driving versus what they were driving. I was completely miserable inside. I believed that my life was a hot mess compared to everyone else, which sucked the joy out of me and took away my peace. If you see this same thing in yourself, you must make a conscious effort to end these types of thoughts. When you compare yourself to other people, you're setting yourself up for a negative cycle of thinking that is really hard to break. Resist with all of your might the urge to let other people's perceived brightness and successes in their lives blind you to the light and talents that you already have and bring into the world. What others have and do is based on the path that they are walking at the time and your own path is most likely very different from theirs. I guarantee you that those people that you are comparing yourself against have their own struggles in life. Make time for yourself to celebrate all that is good and special about you and what you contribute to the world and appreciate all that you have right now. Doing so will break the cycle of comparison and will bring you joy and peace.

Take some time to slow down and enjoy your life. From a young age, I was taught that getting things done quickly was a good thing. This transferred into my adult life where I found myself always being in a rush to get things done. I believed that everything had to be done right now and that there was no time to wait. What I didn't understand at the time was that if I would have slowed down just a bit, I would have been more effective because I wouldn't have made some of the silly mistakes that I made, which were stressful, killed my joy and made me look bad. If you are noticing the same thing in yourself, make an effort to take a step back and slow down just a bit. You'll be much more successful in the long run and you'll find joy in what you're trying to accomplish.

Our culture promotes busyness as a badge of honor. I'm sure you've been in situations where others are telling you how busy they are—likely with a distinct satisfaction. This is where the illusion of busyness fools you into believing that you're doing the right thing if you're constantly tired and stressed. I, too, fell into this trap and it was miserable. You don't need to have your daily calendar packed full of things to accomplish in order to be successful and to have a meaningful life. Rushing around from one meeting to the next or going from one thing to the next only frazzles you, making it almost impossible to be effective and to have joy. Slow down and do things that carry positive meaning for you. Savor each and every moment that comes into your life because once those moments are gone, you'll never have them again. Remind yourself that experiencing the journey that you're on is half of the fun. When you focus on slowing down and take the time to soak in everything around you, you can't help but to be at peace and full of joy.

Another way that your joy can be stolen from you is when you find yourself spending time replaying past events in your mind. I used to find myself dwelling on some perceived slight that I believed someone had directed my way, or second-guessing decisions I had made. These types of thoughts would often come in the middle of the night, waking me from a deep sleep so that I could ruminate on them for hours before eventually falling back asleep just in time for the alarm to sound. The only thing that was accomplished was that I was robbed of sleep, which made me cranky and tired the next day, and my exhaustion kept the negative thought cycle going. You may notice yourself experiencing the same thing, but remember this. The past is just that - the past. Life is lived moment by moment and you can never be completely sure what's going to happen next, and each situation that you will face will require a different reaction. You can remember and learn from how you responded in the past, but the key to keeping your joy alive is to not spend too much time dwelling there. Don't live your life in a state of regret because there is no way that you can change what has already happened.

Resist planning every minute of your day

Have you ever been around someone who is a planner? These are the folks who live their life by their calendars and also have to have every single minute detail of their lives planned out. Before you planners think I'm making fun of you, take a breath and come along with me. I really believe in my soul that when you spend too much time planning and trying to be in control, your focus is distracted away from what's going on in front of you at any given moment. You are also missing out on the positive spontaneous things that might pop up. You could be missing a moment of joy and be completely oblivious to the fact that you missed it! I'm all about planning, but let's be honest, life is going to unfold just as it will and there's absolutely nothing that you or your calendar can do to stop it. There are simply too many unknowns lurking around the corner that can make a shambles of even the most airtight plans, and when these unknowns happen, you just may end up in a spiral of thinking that kills your joy. If you want to experience true joy, loosen up on the reins a little and simply let life unfold just as it will. Who knows, even if things don't work out like you thought they would, you just may find some humor in what becomes. Who doesn't get some joy out of that?

The thoughts that take away your joy may not be exactly the same as the examples that I've discussed, but the effect is still the same. If you don't make an effort to get in front of them, they will unrepentantly steal joy and peace from your life. Your thoughts are always swirling around in your mind without you even recognizing how they are affecting your day to day life and you may not even realize that they're there because you're so used to them being there. Remember when I mentioned previously that I check in with myself several times per day to see how I'm feeling? During those check-ins, I'm stepping out of my head and acting as an observer of how my thoughts are affecting me. In my mind, I'm imagining that I am standing off to the right side of myself, looking at each thought as it enters my mind. Then I step back and let each thought dissipate without attaching any kind of emotion at all to any of them. Remain neutral when looking at your thoughts. Doing this is key to taking away any power that your thoughts may lord over you because most of the time your thoughts are telling you something that isn't true. Take back your power by letting them go. As you continue to do this, it will become second nature to you, putting you on a path to joy and peace.

Have faith to have joy

There isn't one person on the planet, including you, who will not face challenges, hardships and trials. Without joy, it will not only take you longer to get over these events, but you also risk becoming mired in a thought cycle that will keep you cemented in a negative loop. Have you ever found yourself in the presence of someone who isn't all that joyful? I'm sure that you already know the type of person that I'm talking about. The air feels heavy, your interactions with them can be awkward and you begin to feel exhausted around them. These types of people seem like they're under a tremendous amount of strain and tension in their lives, and their lack of joy negatively impacts how you feel.

Let's contrast those types of people with how it feels to be around someone who is full of joy. Because joyful people are less prone to complaining, they lift up those that are around them. Joy is also contagious, and joyful people attract more joy because they make other people feel good. Joyful people also like to laugh, and through this laughter they can bond with others, which makes everyone feel connected and satisfied.

Think back to a time in your life where something happened that sapped your joy and then fast forward to where you are right now. You're still living and breathing and I bet that you are in a much better spot today than you were then. Life does actually have a way of working things out for the best. When I lost my last job, I thought that my world had ended. I was mired down in that thought for a long while. The unwavering faith that I had in myself to find a solution to this challenge eventually lifted me out of that feeling and left me with a deep knowing in my soul that things were going to work out just fine. My faith in a bright and positive outcome to my situation is what brought you and me together through the pages of this book, and I couldn't be more joyful to be spending this time with you.

When you are faced with a challenge or hardship, start by having a strong and unbending faith that things are going to work out just fine, because they will. You will feel empowered, which will give you the impetus to begin making the necessary adjustments that fuel positive change in your situation. You'll find new and different thoughts and ideas to act on entering your mind, which will excite you and fill you with joy. Have faith in yourself and let your unending well of joy offer positive benefits in your life.

The benefits of activating joy in your life

By now, I hope you understand the link between your thoughts and joy. It's tough to focus on joy when you're neck deep in the busyness and craziness of your life and the demands of your job. Believe me, I get it. It's much easier to focus on those things that keep you feeling out of sorts because that's what you're used to do doing. It doesn't have to remain this way, because just like you have allowed your mind to focus only on those things, you can also discipline your mind to focus on joy. These things are not mutually exclusive. When you train yourself to focus on bringing joy into your mind, you naturally take away the sharp edges of your daily challenges and you then naturally receive a whole host of benefits that you may not be thinking about just yet. Let's go through some of them together.

The benefits of joy

When you have joy, you eliminate stress and fear. This is what gives you the power to make the tough decisions. When you are joyful, your intuition gets a boost, and this helps you to confidently and fearlessly power through your life. This also eliminates any stress that you may be experiencing as you weigh your options during the decision-making process. You will also see a reduction in your stress levels because you won't be taking everything so seriously anymore. Remember that most of what you fear doesn't even come true, and using joy to help you through the tough times helps eliminate stress.

Joyful people are more attractive. Most people love a genuine smile over a frown any day. When you're smiling, you're beaming out to the world that you are an optimistic and positive person, which is attractive to everyone. As you activate your joy, you will notice that more and more people will want to be around you.

Joy provides more success at your job. Everyone likes working with someone who tackles their work with joy. When you bring a joyful approach to your work, you are better at performing your work and meeting your deadlines. You are also better at keeping your coworkers and customers happy, which might also help you land that next big success that you've been waiting for.

Joy makes you healthy. All of us are aware that exercise and eating right is really good for us, but, if you're like most, the habit of good exercise and eating right runs in fits and starts. If you're not in the habit of pursuing these types of habits and wish to adopt this for yourself, try activating your joy as a propellant to a new and healthy routine. When your baseline state is one of joy, you are more likely to be interested in optimizing your physical health, which will help you to make conscious efforts to make time for exercise and to choose healthy foods to eat.

Joy helps you sustain feeling good inside. Have you ever noticed that when you are joyful, you feel really good inside? Feeling good usually comes from achieving a level of success in some area of your life and this success doesn't necessarily have to come from your career. It can come from actively engaging in something that you're interested in and that you also have fun doing. I personally take great joy and feel successful when I volunteer my time, cook a nice meal or even take my dog for his twice daily walks. These simple actions help to elevate the level of success that I feel that I've achieved each day. That feels really good to me. Whatever you decide to do that helps you to feel successful and experience sustained good feelings inside of yourself works, so choose something that you like to do and stick with it. You'll notice the good feelings that well up inside of you

Joy helps you laugh more. Take notice of how you feel after you have a really good laugh. When you laugh, your body releases endorphins into your bloodstream that send good feelings through you. It makes you want to laugh more, and you should. Allow yourself to have a real good belly laugh sometimes and notice the positive effect that it has on cementing your joy.

When you are able to experience the benefits that activated joy brings into your life, you notice that it becomes easier to have joy as a baseline state. What you give out to the world always comes back to you and when you are joyful, you start to notice that people respond to you differently and more positively. People naturally want to help other people who are filled with joy. Being joyful is contagious and has a compounding effect that quickly spreads to other people. It also draws more people to you and expands your social circles, which opens up new ways of seeing, understanding and connecting with the world.

Five suggestions to activate your joy

- *Purposely take yourself out of your comfort zone and make room for something new in your life. When you allow yourself to have new experiences, you are opening the door for joy to come in. Resist falling back on the same old way of doing things and revolutionize your life by adding some variety to it. Plan a vacation to a new and unusual destination, make a meal that requires ingredients that you don't normally use or take that class that you've always wanted to take. The sense of success and satisfaction that you will gain will spark your joy.*

- *Make a list of things that bring you joy and try to incorporate those things into your life more often. As you do, there will be more opportunities to add new and exciting items to try to your list, which will keep the cycle of joy going.*

- *Show kindness to others. We'll be talking about this further in chapter 8, but remember that when you make other people feel good, you will also find yourself feeling good, and this will bring you immense joy. You can activate joy by expressing simple kindnesses to others that you come across in your normal day. Pay someone a compliment, give a stranger a smile or hold the door open for someone, for example. When you do so, immediately take notice of how joyous you feel inside. It's that joy that will make you want to continue to offer kindness to everyone you meet.*

- *Learn how to say no more often. Do you ever feel like you have too many things going on and that you are unable to keep up with all of them? If so, it's time to simplify things in order to clear a space for joy. Clear your mental space by only spending your precious time on the things that you are most passionate about and then let the other things go. Don't allow yourself to feel guilty for saying no to anything that doesn't bring you joy. It's through this active cultivation of your time that you will activate and sustain your joy.*

- *Spend more time with happy and joyful people. Develop your tribe carefully, filling it with those that are happy and supportive. Limit or even end your time with any who are jealous and judgmental. Their opinions of you simply don't matter. When you're around people who are filled with joy, it can't help but rub off on you and make you feel good. This gives positive momentum to you sharing joy with other people and keeps the momentum going.*

Joy helps you tackle life's challenges with ease and grace and draws other people to you. By making the conscious decision to activate joy in your life, you are creating a life that includes health, fulfillment and peace.

CHAPTER 5

Activate Generosity and Feel Good

I n the introduction to this book, I suggested that as you progress through the chapters, you will begin to see how complementary each of these human values are to one another. When activated, they will have their own individual positive side effects that you will experience, but there is one bonus side effect that each of them has in common, which is that they will help you feel good inside. When you make the conscious choice to activate and conduct your life by living within the human values that already exist within you, you align yourself with the true essence of your spirit, which always feels good no matter what is occurring around you.

A great way to align yourself with your spirit is through acts of generosity, which means acting in a way that promotes another person's well-being. No matter how you choose to express your generosity to someone, you will notice that your heart fills with the joy we discussed in the last chapter. Achieving a permanently activated mindset of generosity only requires you to consciously change your thoughts to direct your attitude toward being generous. When you act generously, you are essentially acting in service to other people, which makes it complementary to love. It is through these acts of service that you ignite within yourself feelings of contentment, connection and meaningful contribution, which feels good and pushes you to continue acting on your new generous mindset.

When I was first beginning to learn how to activate generosity in myself, I stumbled across the following quote from Anne Frank: "No one has ever become poor by giving." This quote gave me pause. I interpret it as her saying that there is already plenty of everything for everyone, and that when you are generous, what you give away comes back to you many times over. To her, generosity does not entertain the concept of lack because it already fully understands that there is enough of everything to go around. Anne Frank's well-known background makes this quote even more powerful. Tragedy came upon her and her family, because despite others' best efforts to keep them hidden, they were eventually found and were subsequently transferred to the Auschwitz concentration camp. Anne and her sister were then later separated from their parents and were sent alone to the Bergen-Belsen concentration camp, where they both eventually succumbed to Typhus. She witnessed atrocities that other humans visited upon her and the other people in that concentration camp, but I believe that she stood steadfast in her beliefs surrounding generosity. She understood its power on a deep level.

Why you need generosity

The digital age that we're living in right now is one of the best times for getting information easily and quickly. Whatever you want to know is right at your fingertips and can be accessed via your smartphone or your tablet, but it comes at a cost: a degradation of interpersonal skills. The next time that you're out and about, see for yourself by taking notice of the number of people who are checked out, staring at their screens. I believe that this is the main contributor to the feelings of loneliness and isolation that are being experienced in the world today. Social platforms that contribute to hate and vitriol are doing their part in creating and driving divisions between people, which is having a negative impact on society's ability to thrive and develop the deep personal connections that everyone needs to survive. When you add stressful work schedules and never-ending family responsibilities to the mix, you're left with an environment that does not promote generosity and service.

This is perilous, because human beings need one another and they also need to be needed in order to thrive. The need to be needed is one of the most fundamental desires that you have, and when you are generous toward others, you satisfy this need. Studies have shown that when you are generous, your stress level goes down, your physical health gets a boost, and depression is kept at bay. It has even been suggested that generosity increases your lifespan. It also helps you develop new connections with other people and improves the existing relationships that you already have. This is because you accept the people that you're being generous with just as they are, making you view them more positively, strengthening your connection with them.

The key to a successful generous mindset is to expect to receive nothing in return for your efforts. You're engaging in this selfless act because you want to do so. Notice how you feel inside when you do this. You feel good, right? This feeling is key to continuing your practice, but there is a bit of a selfish motivation to it as well. The more generous you are, you'll notice how generosity comes back to you. I promise you that you will receive more generosity in the end than you give, and this is what makes activating your generosity such a great thing. It's a self-fulfilling cycle that knows no bounds because it's already inside each one of us in an unlimited supply. Give it a try and see how it makes you and the recipients of your generosity feel.

Generosity in action

Generosity can arrive in many forms. For some, it might mean giving money to or volunteering with organizations that support people who are in need. Many nonprofits that help communities would not exist if it weren't for the generous contributions of generous people sharing their time and money. You may also see generosity in action on the streets or at your local stoplights where people roll down their car windows to offer money to those who are less fortunate than them. While there are many debates on whether giving money to a panhandler is a good thing or not, please keep the following in mind: If you are questioning or attempting to direct how this person should be using the money that you are offering to them, you are not in congruence with the spirit of generosity.

You may have your own practice of generosity, by freely giving your time through volunteering, performing community related work projects, making time to help a sick friend or to simply listen to someone who needs a lending ear. The opportunities for you to be generous are limited only by your imagination and they don't have to necessarily involve money. Generosity comes from your intent and your actions, and anytime that you consciously match up your generous intent with action behind it, you become a force for good not only for yourself but for others.

I've been lucky to have been on the receiving end of another's generosity many times, and I have also watched in silent awe of people who have selflessly performed generous acts for others, and both have significant positive impacts. I'd like to share with you examples of both of these so that you can see for yourself how wonderful they are.

I've already told you how I once unexpectedly lost my job, which required me to step out of my comfort zone to learn how to effectively network with other people and organizations. It had been a long time since I needed to look for a job, so I was a bit rusty and uncomfortable with doing it and I was really surprised how the mechanics of a job search have changed. Through a networking group that I was a member of, I met a woman named Carol who works for a large organization that I was interested in learning more about. Carol is known as the job whisperer in this organization, though her actual job isn't in recruiting. She does this on her own time and makes time in her hectic schedule to help those who are interested in landing a position with her company. She meets with people mostly during her lunch hour, and it's not uncommon for her to use all of her lunch hours each week to meet with candidates and to help them get a foot in the door. She made time to meet with me for lunch one day where she offered up some tips and tricks that I could use in my search. She even offered to make personal phone calls on my behalf to hiring managers who posted jobs within her company that I was interested in. I sensed in her an abundance of generosity that I have never experienced in anyone else. She barely knew me, yet she was willing to stick her neck out on my behalf, which is something that you don't see very often. Why does she do these things? Because they make her feel good. She is a naturally generous person who wants to help others because she believes in her soul that it's the right thing to do. As time passed, our networking relationship grew into a close friendship. I've received countless invitations to her home for barbecues, lunch and holiday gatherings and I am so lucky to know this wonderful family. I never would have believed that a negative event fraught with so much stress and doubt would have turned out to be so positive in this way, all because of Carol's generous nature.

You may remember from Chapter 1 the affiliation that I have with the Ronald McDonald House. This organization perfectly aligns with my desire to do be of service to others because I have a real soft spot for children, especially children who are injured or are ill. Each December, Ronald McDonald House holds a radio-thon to help raise money for the organization and a popular local radio station and their announcers come into the building and broadcast live, asking the community for donations. There is a phone bank along with several volunteers who start answering the phones as early as 6AM. Even at that early hour, there's an elevated sense of anticipation and excitement in the air that is palpable. Usually, there are a few members of the community who are interviewed live for their donations or for the good acts that they do in support of Ronald McDonald House.

This past December, a young man named Gavin showed up with his mother. Gavin is in the 5th grade, but he is an old soul. He is chock full of wisdom and he has a generous mindset that I've never witnessed before in a person his age. Throughout the year, Gavin helps his family by cleaning their horse stalls as well as their home and he then saves the allowance that he earns to buy teddy bears for the children that are staying at the Ronald McDonald house during the Christmas holiday. While he was being interviewed live and on the air about his good deeds, you could have heard a pin drop because everyone in the room was mesmerized by his words, staring in awe at this wise young man. It appeared that the same thing was occurring with those listening to his interview on the radio because every one of the phones stopped ringing during his time on the air. Gavin taught all of us in that room and in the community a valuable lesson about generosity that day. How he clearly understands this and the importance of sharing it with others at such a young age is a mystery to me, but all of the lives that he has touched are better because of him.

Through these examples of generosity in action, you can decide for yourself what you can do to be of service to others in some way. The key is to just do it and let the positive feelings and momentum that you experience be the inspiration for you to continue. It doesn't really matter how you do it, so use your imagination and make your actions ones of generosity. You'll be glad that you did and the world and you will benefit from it.

Barriers to generosity

When you adopt a mindset of generosity, you are matching your thoughts with your intent to create positive action in service to others. The giving of your time or of your money is generous by default, but you only truly reap the rewards of generosity when you really feel from your heart that you want to do it. You should recognize that heartfelt feeling before even offering up your generous deeds. As your thoughts and your behaviors match up, you activate loving and generous energy inside of you, which feels good and makes you want to continue. There are traps that you can fall into, however, that can create impediments to generosity. Sometimes they present themselves without you being consciously aware of them.

When you offer up your generosity by looking for an approval or a thank you, you're not really being generous. That's a quid pro quo, which is definitely not an act of generosity. If you require someone to throw their gratitude your way for doing something good, you really aren't being generous at all. Remember, generosity comes without expectation of receiving anything in return, including a thank you or a reward.

When you offer your generosity as a way of keeping up with the generous acts that a neighbor or a friend is offering, that is not really being generous either. Being generous isn't a contest, and if you're treating it as such, you're better off not doing anything. Remember, it's the intent behind your actions that determines how generous you really are, so act on your generous impulses because you really want to do so, not because of a perceived social construct or competition.

If you have jealousy or envy in your thoughts, your mindset is one of perceived lack. Lack and generosity are mutually exclusive. If you're envious or jealous of someone, these types of thoughts shut down your ability to be of service to anyone else. Keep in mind that all of us are on our own journey in life, and this includes the things that we have and don't have, so when you believe that someone has more than you, be truly happy for them and move the thoughts of perceived lack out of your mind. You will then notice that your thoughts toward everyone naturally become more generous.

Recently, I was at a social gathering, and as I was mingling around the room, I stumbled into a conversation with a group of people who were discussing the number of panhandlers at stoplights in our city. For the most part, the comments were fairly neutral, and some were even compassionate, but ultimately, judgement creeped in with some talking about how unseemly it was that someone was begging for money, proudly proclaiming that they refused to give to able bodied people that could work and make their own way. I quietly exited the conversation because I became uncomfortable with what I was hearing. When you find yourself in a situation where you are faced with another asking you for money, you don't necessarily have to give them money. But why not offer them a generous thought?

You could silently wish them well and pray that they are able to exit from their unfortunate situation soon. Generosity doesn't necessarily have to involve money, and by sending a generous thought to someone, you are silently recognizing that they are human beings and that they deserve the same opportunities that you already enjoy without ostracizing them.

Our culture promotes the acquiring of as much of everything as you possibly can, which can give you a temporary feeling of having enough. Before you know it, that feeling is gone and you move on to the next thing that you have your sights set on. Beginning right now, think about your life in a different way. You really don't need as much as you think you do in order to thrive. Just by virtue of being alive, you are already getting everything that you truly need. This includes the sunlight that warms the planet, the food that keeps you alive and healthy and the oxygen that fills your lungs and keeps your heart beating. You're already surrounded by generosity without having to do anything to receive it. Turn that receiving into action and share your own generosity with those already around you.

How generous people think

In each of the roles that I've held with various nonprofits, I've had opportunities to meet many of the generous people who have been a part of these causes, either through the donation of their time or their money. I've noticed some similarities in how they view the world.

Generous people understand that there are a lot of problems in the world, but they aim their focus and efforts on what they can do within their circle of influence. They find meaning and reward in their efforts, even if those efforts only help one person. They also have a tremendous amount of trust in other people. If they are giving financial resources, they automatically assume that those funds will be used for their best purpose. They know in their hearts that what they give now will have a positive impact on the future of that organization or person and they want to be a part of that. Generous people don't have an "accumulation" mentality and are happy to live their lives with less. They realize that by living with less, they are able to give more of their resources to others. And, finally, generous people understand that life is short. You only get a finite amount of time to make your mark on the world, so why not do it with your heart cheerfully and passionately?

These examples prove again that generosity has a positive impact not only on the person receiving the benefits, but also on the person who is doing the giving. You too can shift your view just like other generous people have by taking advantage of the many opportunities in your community or social network to give your time or financial resources. You'll be happier because of it.

Five suggestions for you to activate your generosity

- *If you want to start donating to causes, start small. By starting with a small amount, you ease your way into the game by giving what you're most comfortable with and what suits your financial picture at that particular time. By starting small and remaining in the habit of giving as often as you can, it becomes easier as time goes on, and you'll notice that you most likely won't even miss what you're giving away. Don't feel bad about only giving just a couple of dollars if that's all you can do. The recipient of your money will be grateful for it, no matter how much it is.*

- *Give your time to a charity that interests you. Today, people are more pressed for time than ever, which has had a negative impact on charities that depend on volunteer work. You might be surprised by how much free time you have to offer when you take stock of how you conduct your normal day. Spend one less hour scrolling through social media, for example, and then give that hour of time away. The benefit to you is that you receive much needed human connection, and when you realize the positive impact that your good act generates and how good it makes you feel, you will be compelled to continue with your generous acts.*

- *Be a gracious receiver of gifts. Most people get great joy out of giving, so don't deny them that joy by downplaying their generous acts to you. Give them a heartfelt thank you and accept their offering. I know that this can be hard because I've struggled with it myself. For most of my life, I had a very difficult time with accepting others' generosity because I didn't believe that I deserved it. If you experience the same feelings, think back to what I wrote earlier about humans needing one another to survive, and make the effort to gracefully accept generous efforts that come your way. You'll feel good inside when you see the positive reaction that your appreciation offers, and this will jumpstart the activation of your own generosity.*
- *Make the effort to make your generosity meaningful. When expressing your generosity to those where you choose to give a gift, give something that is meaningful and special to that person. This tells them that you've taken the time to get to know them and to understand what their likes and dislikes are. This also gets you into the habit of taking the focus off of yourself and redirecting your thoughts on how you can always serve other people.*
- *Keep your compassion activated. Go back to chapter 1 and again practice the suggestions to activate your compassion so that it remains alive within you. Compassion and generosity go hand in hand, and when you're com-*

passionate to other people, it becomes second nature to be generous.

When you activate a mindset of generosity, what you are asking is how you can best serve the world. By being generous, you receive back many times over the same generosity that you give, so keep it activated by adopting a service mindset. Give without asking for anything in return and refrain from seeking recognition for your efforts. You will feel good and develop positive meaning and connection in your life.

CHAPTER 6

Activate Courage and End Fear

n chapter 3, we imagined how you can live a fulfilling life by adopting an attitude of gratitude. Now, I'd like to ask you to do a similar exercise, except this time, imagine what your life would look like if you were living fearlessly. Imagine yourself confidently and effortlessly moving through your days, achieving anything that you want. This will require you to reprogram your mind so that you can eliminate outdated ways of thinking that keep you from living courageously. You already have the ability to accomplish anything you want, but it takes courage to reach your hand out and grab it. If you can harness your courage in a way that serves you, I promise that the rewards you will reap will be worth it. Your confidence and energy levels will soar and you will quickly realize that you really have nothing at all to be fearful about. You will understand that you have the ability to accomplish any task that you take on by effortlessly tapping into your inner courage. As a bonus, you may even find a new purpose for your life that you find exciting and fulfilling! But before we dive into how to be courageous, let's look at the role that fear plays in your life.

Fear's role in your life

As I'm writing this chapter, the world is living through the COVID-19 Pandemic. Because there is so much that is unknown about this disease, its effects and how long it may last, many people are fearful, acting out in ways that they normally wouldn't. Panic buying from grocery stores is occurring, leaving shelves bare and with not enough left for others. Schools, businesses, and restaurants are being closed to help stop the spread, which have spurred demonstrations as people voice their dissent against state governments for not lifting stay at home orders. As demands for services and products begin to erode, many are losing their jobs and their health insurance to a market that hasn't seen such drastic drops in activity since the Great Depression. The "normal" way of doing things and living life has been challenged, and this is forcing all of us to contemplate and face our fears in order to find our new normal.

Have the recent events around the pandemic made you evaluate any fears that you have? It takes a little bit of thought and effort to turn inward in order to assess what you are afraid of, but taking that time will assist you in understanding which fears are illusions and which are real and require your attention to overcome them.

COVID forced me to evaluate some of my own fears because I caught the illness while writing this book, contracting it just as the outbreak was beginning to spread in the United States. The onset of the condition occurred rapidly and I don't recall any other time in my life where I was as sick as I was with this terrible disease. My symptoms included dry cough, extreme weakness and muscle aches that made me feel as if I was on fire from the inside out. But the most troubling symptom was that my memory was negatively impacted. I couldn't remember what I had for breakfast thirty minutes afterwards and I struggled to remember to do even the simplest tasks on the days where I felt energetic enough to tackle them. I was quite fearful that my full memory would never return. Thankfully, with enough time and rest, I eventually recovered and began to feel like my usual self again, but it took 9 tough weeks from start to finish to finally get there.

After COVID, I felt a sense of renewal, but having that difficult experience made me pause and reflect on some of the fears that had also been holding me back for a long time. Some of those fears now seemed tame in comparison. In my mind, I had just battled and overcome a serious illness, and while I wasn't overly confident about accomplishing that, I believed that if I could overcome COVID, I could certainly dig in and finally conquer some of my own fears.

One of the fears that I held was in asking for what I want. I was always elated and willing to help when someone would ask something of me, but I didn't feel right asking for the same in return. I'm not a timid person, but I preferred to go it alone and figure it out on my own. When I finally summoned the courage to rise above that fear and to ask for help, the world didn't come crashing down around me, as I had feared that it would. Instead, the exact opposite occurred. I was met with openness and understanding and my connections with those who I asked for help deepened. I learned that people do want to help and be of assistance because doing so makes them feel good. When you show a little vulnerability and let another be of assistance to you, it goes a long way to developing a strong and lasting connection with them.

You don't have to experience a life-altering event in order to start the process of overcoming your fears.

You can do it right now, by first understanding what your fears are and then evaluating how they may be slowing down the desired outcomes that you want to see in your life. No one can go it alone, and we all need each other to survive and thrive. Don't let your ego get in the way of your growth and cause you to shrink down. Your ego exploits these types of situations, which then affects what you believe about yourself and how you respond. You can either respond in a positive and courageous way or you can hand your power over to your ego and let it control your life. Anytime that you give your power away because of fear, you stop making decisions from your heart. By shrinking down and disappearing behind fear, you limit your opportunities to establish needed connections with others, and this has a negative impact on developing true meaning in your life.

Common Fears

Every single one of us have something that we are scared of. You may believe that your fears are unique to just you, but you would be surprised at how many others share the same fears that you do. Being fearful is perfectly normal, but you can't let your fears stop you from living your best life and achieving all that you can. You must overcome your fears if you're going to accomplish all that you set out to do and the first step in dealing with them is to recognize what they are so that you can develop a plan to face them head on and progress.

Another of my biggest fears was that I was really afraid of being ridiculed. It affected my life for a long time and it held me back, causing me to make myself as small as I could. I placed myself in the background because I believed that I was doing something in the wrong way or, worse yet, that I couldn't even do it at all. I was fearful of being ridiculed when giving presentations at work. While speaking, all I saw was a sea of lifeless faces before me, just waiting to pounce. Looking back now, it was a silly fear because nothing bad ever happened, but at the time it was debilitating. Not believing in myself would cause me to make careless mistakes, and made that fear become a self-fulfilling prophecy. Once I stopped underestimating and began trusting in myself, I went on to become well-versed at delivering presentations.

Please remember this: never underestimate your power to tackle an objective or the power of your thoughts. Every single one of us have had some ridicule hurled at us at some point and it can feel paralyzing and humiliating, but remember that those events speak nothing about your value and what you have to offer. Simply because you are here right now, you hold much more value than you believe you do. You are loved beyond measure.

History has provided a good lesson on how much any one person can accomplish in spite of ridicule. Orville and Wilbur Wright were able to harness the power of flight, but they faced many challenges in their quest to get their enterprise fully running. These two men, who didn't have high school degrees, learned the physics of flying and then proceeded to build their airplanes themselves with lots of sweat and dedication. In addition to technical difficulties, they faced a lot of ridicule and scrutiny from the public. Some people said that once they did finally get their airplane airborne that they would never be able to stop it while others implied that they would fall right out of the sky and crash back to the ground, destroying the airplane and ending their lives. These comments didn't stop them, and they were still able to summon the courage to continue on to realize the attainment of their dream. They may have been fearful that what their critics said would come true, but they forged ahead anyway, which defines courage perfectly. The only way out of fear is through it, and courage is what gets you across the finish line.

You may also notice that you are dealing with a fear of failure. I also used to suffer from this fear, and it held me back in so many ways. If I was fearful of tackling something that needed to be done, I would run far away from it and allow others to complete it so that

I could alleviate my anxiety. During these episodes, I sometimes felt like I was displaced from my body, acting as an observer of my life from a far away, safe vantage point rather being an active participant in the outcome. I didn't feel like I was connected to myself or anyone else and it was a terrible, lonely feeling. I learned that in order to deal with the things that you label as failures in your life, you have to change the way that you think about failure.

You can view failure through a positive lens and remove its negative power over you. Think back to times in the past where public figures, whose lives are almost always front and center to all of us, have "failed" in some way and yet risen back up again to the same level of or to even more success than they enjoyed before. You may even remember seeing the same thing happening with your friends or family members. You want to know what the main difference is between those that overcome their supposed failures and those who become defeated? It is simply that they don't view failure as a reason to shrink down and disappear from life. They take a step back and use that time to contemplate what has happened to them, to learn from their particular situation and then turn it around in a way that positively serves them. When viewed in this manner, anything that may cause you to "fail" can be described as a change in direction that helps you recalibrate your life and successfully live in your real purpose.

You may also find yourself dealing with a fear of success. One afternoon, I was having a very heartfelt conversation with a person who had recently been elevated to an executive level position at a nonprofit that I support. I asked them how their life had changed since beginning their new role. I learned from this person that, while they were happy to have had their hard work rewarded in such a positive way, they didn't feel like they were ready for the level of responsibility they were taking on. They abhorred the idea of going to donor meetings and dinners where they would be under the spotlight and where they would be expected to shake hands and make small talk with the people that supported them. Having responsibility for meeting financial targets necessary to keep the doors open made them tremble with fear and they were wracked with anxiety. More importantly, they had a fear of disappointing or letting other people down. This person admitted that they had a fear of success.

This fear is a lot more common than you think. On the outside, someone may come across as calm and ready to accept any challenge, but inside, they're a nervous wreck. Fear of success is rarely about becoming successful, rather, it's usually more about being fearful of the results that success brings. Success brings more money, which you will get used to and then have to maintain, it also brings about success that the organization that you work for will receive and then want to maintain. The pressure of this fear can lead to heightened levels of anxiety and stress, which causes burnout, but can also make you act in ways that can bring your success down. The world needs your talents and your success is a part of the formula for the world to continue to grow and prosper. With your success, you are serving other people for the better and helping them to become successful, too. So, when you find yourself experiencing a fear of success, remind yourself to reflect back on and to think positive thoughts about your past accomplishments. You are a part of something that is much greater than you, and you can use your success to positively contribute to that greater good. I think one of the most important things you can do is to be grateful for the success that may come your way. Practicing gratitude for getting to this point in your life will help put any negative thoughts that you have about it in perspective.

You may also notice that you are dealing with a fear of change. When I was young, I remember frequently hearing the phrase "the only constant is change." At the time, I didn't even know what that meant, but it's meaning became clearer to me as I grew older, and

I didn't like it for one second. I enjoyed the familiar routines of young life, where I always knew what to expect from one day to the next. This idyllic routine set me up for real disappointment as I grew into adulthood. When I went off to college and then moved into the "real" world to work and earn a living, I was so resistant to change that it severely limited my growth and my learning. The innocence of my youth was gone now and I didn't know what do with this new way of being. I had developed a fear of change.

Change is difficult for everyone and it can cause even the emotionally strongest amongst us to begin to feel a bit anxious. It's totally normal to feel this way. What's not beneficial is when fear of change prevents you from moving forward in your life. Change occurs every day - it's the natural order of the Universe. You recognize it when you witness summer giving way to fall, which then gives way to winter. These seasonal changes come whether you want them to or not. Every single material thing that you buy comes into your life, serves its purpose until it doesn't and then moves on out of your life to either be recycled, given away or placed in the trash. You're even going through changes with your physical body right now. You were once a baby and you grow older with each passing day, introducing gray hair and wrinkled skin. Change brings with it endings that you may not be so quick to accept, but thought about in a different way, this ending can represent a new beginning for you.

When I was still working in Corporate America, the frequency and justification of process changes used to be a real thorn in my side. Not only would I have to learn a new way of working, but I'd also have to get my team up to speed on the new changes and there was always resentment and pushback that came from it. What I finally realized was that the old process had once been a new process that past employees had to learn and deal with, and now, it's no longer suitable for the current needs of the business. The new process could represent a new beginning that was full of promise and a new and efficient way of accomplishing tasks. When I presented this concept in this way to my team, there were still those that resisted, but most came aboard and learned the process. Do your best to accept and welcome new changes as a means to try something new in your life and to also learn a new way of doing your work or whatever it is that you're trying to accomplish. When you embrace change, you expand your knowledge that you can then carry with you for the rest of your life. Acting as a change agent also changes the way your mind works and helps you to be innovative and creative when solving problems. By having the courage to accept that change is indeed constant, you invite peace and the ability to successfully thrive into your life.

Fear can be positive

Being fearful can be unsettling, and when you let your imagination run wild with it, you begin to drum up all types of disastrous scenarios or outcomes that you believe will happen, all before the thing you fear has come to pass. When I faced my own fears, I learned the following two things.

Fear can propel you to take action. As I was in the middle of writing this book, I developed a fear of finishing it. My fear was rooted in how I believed my message would be received by readers. Before the book was even finished, I was convinced that no one would like the book, which thwarted my progress. I overcame this fear by pushing myself to finish writing it, which ultimately made me feel great. By taking action, my anxiety melted away and I believed in myself, and this gave me the confidence to forge ahead.

Fear can also be an indicator that you're getting out of your comfort zone, stretching yourself to do or learn something new. Again, while writing this book, I kept reminding myself that I'm just a Finance guy who's never been trained in writing and who is used to working with spreadsheets and slide decks all day. Who do I think I am to take this on? Getting this book into your hands required me to stretch myself to not only do the work, but to also accept help from a lot of intelligent people who have been there every step of the way on this journey. Don't be afraid to try something new. When you break up your normal routine, it's natural to question yourself and to wonder if you can really do it or if what you're doing is even feasible, but keep forging ahead anyway. The payoff comes in increased self-confidence and expanded knowledge.

No one is immune to fear and everyone struggles with it at one time or another. By keeping this top of mind, you will feel motivated to face what you are fearful of and you will build a new base of useful insights that may help you in the future. You're never going to totally eliminate fear, but understanding it and how it affects you will help you keep it under control.

The pitfalls of living in fear

Your relationships with others can be severely damaged when you let fear take over your life. The most common side effect of this fear is that it can create conflict, especially when you lash out at a person who you believe may be pushing you out of your comfort zone. It changes your perception of that person and affects your personal interactions with them in a negative way. Fear can also make you shrink down and appear uneasy in front of other people. Others are able to sense this, making them feel closed and unwilling to open up to you, which can further increase your sense of separation from them. Fear can negatively affect your mental health as well as your physical health, causing depression and disrupting the normal functioning of your body.

Most of the fears that you have never come to fruition anyway. They're products of an overactive imagination. Develop and activate your courage because it gives you the ability to face what you are fearful of and helps you move through it until you're successfully on the other side of a particular fear.

One final note

You are fortunate to have a mind that allows you to think critically about and make decisions on events that affect your everyday life. You alone can determine whether the decisions you make work for or against you. You make these assessments frequently with little information and often without even giving them a second thought, but their impact on you changes as age creeps in and you begin to evaluate your life. It's inevitable that you will think back on and assess how you handled events in your past, considering whether or not you did the things that made you feel fulfilled in your life. I've witnessed this through conversations with relatives or friends who were at the end of or close

to the end of their lives. They all felt immense gratitude and satisfaction for outcomes where they made
decisions that involved risk and uncertainty, where
they had no guarantee of success. Sometimes things
worked out for the best and sometimes they didn't, and
while they experienced satisfaction when things did
work out, they also felt satisfaction when they were
redirected to other avenues that brought them to different, yet fulfilling outcomes.

Keep in mind that things always have a way of
working out for the best. An unplanned outcome
might end up being the most valuable later on. A redi-
rection away from your carefully thought out plan can
indeed be the very thing that you needed the most in
that particular moment of your life. It takes courage
to pursue something in life even when you're fearful of what may happen and it also takes courage to
accept and ride along with the redirections that you
will inevitably face.

So, how can you activate your courage? Read
below so that you can conquer your fears and begin
experiencing more positive outcomes in your life.

Five suggestions to activate your courage

- *Acknowledge your fears and then push through them
  anyway. You have most likely heard it said that in order
  to get over your fear, you have to walk through it. When*

you do this, you gain a better understanding of your capabilities and begin to feel inspired, which will then give your confidence and courage a boost.

- *Strive for objectivity when evaluating your fears. Most of the time, the outcome that you're afraid of never happens, so ask yourself what the worst-case scenario is if what you're fearful of does indeed occur. Will you learn something that you didn't know before? If so, that's a win for you. This will keep you centered on what actually happened rather than making you focus on your feelings.*
- *Take small steps to move out of your comfort zone. Activating courage happens over time, so be patient as you are attempting to do something that scares you. As you successfully complete each step, you'll feel increasing confidence that will sustain you to complete subsequent steps.*
- *Speak up for yourself! Even when it feels difficult to do, do it anyway. Doing so allows other people to see, understand and respect the real you. You'll feel heard, your confidence will grow and your fears will diminish on the spot.*
- *Surround yourself with people who will encourage you to think big about your life and move on from those who squash your desires. Surround yourself with people who think like you do. They will light the candle of courage within you so that you fearlessly achieve your dreams*

Give your all to standing up and staring your fear in the face and then watch it retreat while your confidence soars. Have you ever noticed or admired someone who seems fearless and confident? That person still has things that they are afraid of, but they have the necessary confidence and trust in themselves to successfully deal with them. It's that same confidence and trust that they have in themselves that draws other people to them. This can be your reality, too, and not only will you gain the satisfaction of knowing that you've successfully conquered your fears, you'll feel strongly connected to others, developing satisfying and meaningful relationships. They will eventually look to you for inspiration and guidance and you will feel good because you can help support them. Activate your courage and you will become a successful co-creator of your life. You will no longer need to imagine it because you'll be living it.

CHAPTER 7

Activate Integrity and Live in Your Truth

Your personal integrity is your own unique brand, which defines how others view and react to you. When each decision and action are aligned with well thought out values, you live in your truth by consistently approaching your interactions in an ethical, open and honest manner. The values, or principles that I'm speaking of surround positive ways of treating others and acting from a sense of goodness and always doing the right thing. In the words of Oprah Winfrey, "Real integrity is doing the right thing, knowing that nobody's going to know whether you did it or not." When you conduct yourself in this manner, the way that you respond to the world is positive, thoughtful and calm.

What personal integrity looks like

Living a life of integrity establishes you as someone who is trustworthy and who can always be depended on. It means being viewed by others as someone who has a strong character and is unwavering in their core beliefs. When I think about a person with a high level of integrity, the first picture that comes to my mind is a tall and towering tree. That tree represents strength and is a metaphor for the human equivalent of living firmly rooted in your values. No matter how strong the wind may blow and no matter how much the tree may be pushed back and forth, it always ends up back at its full height. It continues to survive and even thrive, despite conditions that sometimes seem counter to its existence. The same thing can be said about you when you live by your personal principles. You will always face high winds from life's events, but that won't matter when you become like that tall and towering tree. When all of the decisions that you make and all of the actions that you take have the foundation of your principles as their bedrock, your personal integrity remains intact and you naturally thrive in your life.

One of the most influential people who helped me develop my own personal integrity is a manager from one of my former jobs. He was only my leader for about a year and a half, but in that short period of time, he taught me so much about what personal integrity looks like and inspired me to live my life just as he does. He previously had a career in the United States Air Force where he held his own Command at a base in Italy. Upon retiring, he entered the civilian workforce and was leading a newly signed Information Technology contract with the United States Navy. He needed a Business Manager to help him with the contract's finances. When I interviewed with him for the role, I went into the interview expecting someone who was very rigid and tough, but he proved to be the opposite. The interview was relaxed, but he asked difficult and in-depth questions. He expressed an openness and willingness to understand how I would approach solving challenges without being tied to previous ideas that he had developed in his mind.

Fortunately, I landed the job and soon discovered that he was a real stand-up guy with his customers and fellow co-workers. He invited me to attend face to face customer meetings with him and it was almost magical to watch him discuss the challenges that they were facing and strategize how our company could help solve them. He listened calmly and attentively and, when it was his turn to talk, he proposed solutions that could be counted on to bring success and help his customers meet their own goals. There were certainly disagreements, but on those occasions, he listened attentively, first trying to understand what the issue was and then negotiating in good faith on what he could do to mitigate the challenge. He would then bring that information back to his team at the office and include us as a team on the path forward toward a workable solution. While discussing our options, he acted as a referee of sorts, gently redirecting our focus when we went off the rails, while simultaneously praising us for out of the box thinking. Eventually, we would settle on a path forward and, when it came time to start working, he would roll up his sleeves and jump in the trenches with us, acting as a calm and reassuring force, keeping the project on the right path while simultaneously keeping the needs of his team and customers in balance. He stood by his principles of solid customer service, unwavering respect for his team and trusting his gut instinct. He never let an unhappy customer or a dissatisfied employee stop him from pursuing what he knew needed to be done. He was calm, had a reassuring presence, and in an unassuming way, had full command of each challenge. Both his team and his customers loved and respected him, and because of this, he was able to grow his business into a large and profitable enterprise for the company. Today, he is the CEO of a successful organization that provides consulting services, and he is the picture of what personal integrity, looks like. He fully lives in his truth.

I tell you about this important person in my life because my tenure in that role was incredibly influential on how I would set my own agenda going forward. I felt compelled to live by my manager's example and so I spent a great deal of time hashing out in my mind what I wanted my role on this planet to be, which compelled me to develop the principles that I was determined to live the rest of my life by. Principles such as honesty, generosity, compassion and a willingness to help elevate others in their own lives became my own truths that I conduct my life by to this very day. You can do the same thing for yourself. You don't need to be a genius to figure these things out and then develop a personal plan. It does, however, take discipline and a willingness on your part to keep your principles front and center in your thoughts every moment of every day, so that you don't waver. The personal rewards of living in alignment with your values are vast, leading to a life full of satisfaction, meaning and connection.

The rewards of living in your integrity

One of my favorite writers, Jack Canfield, focuses on the underlying theme that you are a unique individual and that you are here to bring your special energy and characteristics into the world. You are very much needed and have a purpose to fulfill that allows you to share your talents and gifts with everyone. You accomplish this by thinking positively and taking action toward achieving your goals.

What happens when you don't give yourself the permission to do this? You live behind a veil that hides who you really are, which causes you to develop limiting beliefs about yourself, and as a result, you fall out of alignment with your soul. Your soul knows the real you, and when you live in ways that are counter to it, a drain on your integrity occurs. This is why you must always go within to your soul's level to really understand the principles of integrity that you want to cultivate for yourself. When you get really clear on the positive principles that you wish to live by and then demonstrate those principles fearlessly, you become a shining light that compels others to act in the same way that you are. You will also receive many rewards for your efforts.

One of the best rewards of living with high personal integrity is that you become authentic. There is no better feeling than knowing deep within your soul that you are showing up in the world in a way that makes you happy and satisfied and that serves others at the same time. It helps you to become more honest with yourself about your life's purpose and it also brightly illuminates the path that you need to take to fulfill your unique purpose. You notice that your life develops a deep personal meaning to you and that you are living outwardly with something good that comes from within you. This is exactly how I viewed my manager. His authenticity came from within and it was very motivating for his team, compelling us to do the best job that we could in order to support his efforts.

You will also notice that you develop a deep level of trust with other people. This is because the words that you speak are backed up with tangible actions and results that others can see and experience for themselves. Others realize that you walk the walk and they then develop trust, respect and connection with you. If, however, your actions speak to the contrary, you will have a difficult time cultivating that trust and connection.

A high level of trust will work in your favor with your career, where you may begin to get new and challenging assignments that expand your knowledge base and bring more money in your paycheck.

Your confidence will also soar as you develop a strong sense of pride that is tied to the positive actions that you take towards others and yourself. You feel really good about what you're doing and how you show up in the world, which increases your self-respect, self-esteem and ultimately your self-confidence. Your connection with other people naturally grows stronger, which further adds more meaning to your life

You will also notice that you become very clear headed when you are faced with making tough decisions in your life. You will effortlessly call upon the deep reservoir of knowledge that you have amassed and the decisions that you have to make will become crystal clear to you. You will stand tall and confident, be more decisive, and most importantly, you will have full trust in yourself with each decision that you make.

Challenges to your integrity

Conducting your life with integrity will inevitably introduce challenges that test your new and improved mindset. Acting with integrity requires vigilance in every situation that you find yourself in so that you can refer back to your values as guidance. Remind yourself of the rewards mentioned previously and the personal level of satisfaction that you will receive by staying on course with the new direction that you've set for yourself and you will naturally settle in to a rhythm of acting with integrity.

One possible challenge to living with integrity is in making assumptions. It's totally natural to make assumptions, each of us does it, but it's important to be aware of the intent that is behind each assumption that you make. Not all assumptions are bad. It's harmless to assume how long it might take you to shop for groceries or to assume that you're going to have a great time at a dinner out with your friends or family. However, your assumptions can be harmful when you make them about a person or a situation without having all of the knowledge necessary to gauge things correctly. I used to struggle with this type of assumption making, finding myself believing things that weren't necessarily true about people that I first met. I based how I thought and felt about a person based on a first impression, without really knowing who they were. This sometimes led me to underestimate them, which then had a negative impact on how I treated them. The opportunity cost to my thinking was the number of connections and friendships that I missed out on because of the quick assumptions that I would make about other people. Eventually, as I activated my integrity, I wised up and turned that thinking around. By doing so, I opened myself to a new world of experiences and connections.

When you have a high level of personal integrity, you always give your all when completing a task and you place a high premium on doing things the right way all of the time. After all, it's your stamp that's on your work effort and you want to be known as being thorough and correct. Sometimes, especially when you're facing multiple deadlines, it's tempting to take a shortcut and fudge your work a little. Before too long, you become tempted to act in the same way over and over again and when you're found out, it compromises your current success and future opportunities. If people believe that they can't trust you and your work, you'll miss out on future assignments that showcase your skills and experience and create growth personally or in your career.

You've seen on the news how a lack of integrity can affect business. Think back on the Enron scandal. That terrible situation caused the company to fall and also shook Wall Street to its core. The leadership of Enron traded their personal integrity for their own financial success by communicating to regulators that they had holdings that made them appear financially stronger than they really were. This combined with their dishonest accounting practices that were used to hide their large debt and bad assets from investors and creditors caused the company to declare bankruptcy when they were finally found out. The entire company fell to pieces almost overnight and many people lost their livelihoods because of it. All because personal integrity took a back seat to doing the right thing. Success gained without personal integrity is temporary because it doesn't have a solid foundation.

A similar challenge to your personal integrity is in lying. It's tempting to use a lie, even what we call a white lie, to get yourself out of a jam, but the long-term payoff of lying evaporates quickly. If you're willing to lie once, you'll become willing to do it over and over again, and when you do this, it becomes difficult to keep up with all of the lies that you've told. Eventually, you'll slip up and get caught, and that's when your personal integrity bottoms out. Have the courage to always tell the truth, even when it's uncomfortable, so that you don't risk losing a friendship or relationship over it. You'll be respected in the long run and people will believe and trust you, which opens you up to stronger connections with others.

These potential challenges to your integrity are just a small sampling of what you can expect as you move through your life. When you develop a strong base of principles that you choose to live your life by, and consistently practice them, you have a strong foundation in place to face any challenge to your integrity that will come your way.

Now that you understand some of the rewards and challenges to living a life of high personal integrity, let's talk next about the ways that you can activate integrity for yourself.

Five suggestions to activate your integrity

- *Define the positive principles that you wish to be the foundation of your personal integrity and write them down. Remember, your soul always knows what's right, so let your soul's guidance light your path.*

- *Make a daily habit of reflecting on the principles that you've written down each day before you start your day. This will keep those principles front and center in your mind as you're faced with challenges.*

- *Each time that life tosses an event your way that tests your personal integrity, consider your options based on your principles and then take the time to reflect on which one is most in line with the event. Then respond in congruence with that principle.*

- *Shortly after your response, reflect back on how well it did or didn't go. Ask yourself if it felt good or if you experienced a sense of regret or anxiety. These feelings will let you know if you are in line with your principles and help you make adjustments for the next time.*

- *Keep your integrity alive and well by surrounding yourself with people that you view as high personal integrity individuals. You'll naturally raise the bar on yourself and keep your high personal integrity level intact.*

When you feel as if your integrity is being tested, reflect on the quote from Oprah Winfrey in the opening paragraph of this chapter. It's about doing the right thing, regardless of whether anyone else will know. With activated integrity, you always know what's best to do in situations that present themselves to you, so actively consult with yourself as it relates to your exacting standards of integrity. You'll be living in your own personal truth and experience a life full of trust, meaning and connection with others.

CHAPTER 8

Activate Kindness and Have Lasting Well-being

I n the introduction to this book, I described a very common traffic event that occurred while I was out running errands one day. I credit that event with providing the inspiration to write this book.

While I viewed that person's actions toward me and their fellow drivers as unkind, I was able to tap into my higher self and make the correct choice to move past any thoughts of "getting even." I could have chosen to catch up with them and give them a piece of my mind at the next stop light. That's not something that I would typically do, but I'll admit that the idea did occur to me. What purpose would it have served, anyway? Had I chosen to let their actions get under my skin, that moment would have been churning around over and over in my mind for the rest of the day, building up anger, which would most certainly have impacted how I treated everyone else that I came in contact with that day. This is ego-driven thinking.

You may notice this same type of thinking in yourself sometimes. But when you submit to your ego and let challenging situations affect how you feel and respond, it becomes impossible to extend kindness to other people. The buildup of anger makes you unhappy and your unhappiness makes it difficult to appreciate anything and your interactions with everyone around you suffers. It's a less than optimal cycle of thinking. Unfortunately, some people live out their entire lives this way, but it doesn't have to be like this for you. If you can change the way you think about challenging situations that come up in your life, you will get to a point where these types of events no longer fluster you. Your level of happiness will increase, which has a great effect on the kindness that you offer to others. It feels good to be kind to people, and that good feeling has the greatest impact on your overall sense of well-being. In this chapter, I'll share with you how I learned to increase the kindness that I offered, but first, let's understand the difference between being nice and being kind.

The difference between being nice and being kind

Many of us believe that being nice and being kind are interchangeable, but there are important differences between the two. Being nice comes from what is expected of us to live within societal norms. It's good to be nice, and important to do so, but its benefits are mostly superficial. Being kind is a little different. Kindness comes from your character and lives in your heart. Everyone has kindness in them and it's one of the human values that has its permanence at the core of who you are. Kindness positively serves other people and it promotes a strong sense of well-being within you.

I bet that you currently know or have known people that you would describe as being nice. Nice people are willing to bend over backwards to accommodate and pacify others because they usually can't live with the idea of conflict. They give up on their own needs, always sacrificing themselves in order to keep conflict at bay. They are often taken advantage of, which leads to them being mistreated and perceiving themselves as a doormat, which subsequently makes them very unhappy inside. Before too long, feelings of resentment begin to build and they begin to keep a mental checklist of all of the things that they've done for others, comparing what they've given with what they've received. The resentment can expose itself through explosive outbursts of anger, leaving hurt feelings and compromised relationships in its wake, which makes it impossible to have a strong sense of well-being.

On the other hand, the foundation of a kind person's character is built on a healthy level of confidence and self-esteem. They're not looking for validation by bending over backwards for others. Kind people genuinely give from their heart and they know how to set up boundaries to their kindness so that they don't get taken advantage of. They know how to say no when they need to and are genuinely happy on the inside. Kind people have a very strong sense of self-respect and they take care of themselves first, which provides the foundation for their happiness. People who are kind offer their generosity to others, which contributes positively to their overall sense of well-being.

When I began to observe my own behavior with others, I realized that I was consistently nice, but maybe not as kind as I could be. I was OK with being nice, but I began to realize it came at a price to me, keeping me from living authentically. I accepted situations that I didn't like in order to keep the peace, and I was reluctant to challenge unappetizing situations to me when I needed to. I was unhappy and I couldn't figure out why. It took a very angry outburst toward someone that I was very close with to finally open my eyes and to understand how much my being nice was really hurting me and my relationships with other people. My self-esteem and my confidence were low, and when I began to take conscious action to build them up, I learned how to give from my heart because I wanted to, not because I felt like I had to in order to get approval. I did this by activating my kindness following the suggestions that you'll see at the end of this chapter.

Why we need kindness

Humans are social creatures and we have the ability to express care and concern for one another. We need one another to survive, yet this need for survival doesn't necessarily translate into treating one another with kindness. Being selfish and competitive are products of our egos. Our egos tell us that if we have more of anything, that we're better than those that don't have those same things, and this creates separation between us that shuts off kindness.

This isn't why we're here. Everything on this planet is connected, and if we take the time to understand just how interconnected we are with one another, kindness is effortless to achieve. What happens to one of us affects all of us, and when we band together to overcome challenges, we thrive. When we understand just how interconnected we really are, it motivates us to be inclusive, to accept one another for who we are and promotes our growth, which then positively impacts everyone. All of this has its roots in kindness.

Embrace kindness and stop being so nice

One of the reasons that I was a people pleaser who would bend over backwards for others is because I didn't believe in myself very much. I viewed myself as average or maybe even below average. I was my own worst critic. My level of self-love, which we talked about in chapter 2, was non-existent, and I believed that I had to be overly nice to people in order to get them to like and respond to me. It was unhealthy and exhausting. This view that I held of myself changed when I accidentally ran across a verse from the Chinese Tao Te Ching.

The Tao Te Ching by Lao Tzu is full of timeless wisdom on the nature of life. It consists of 82 verses that have been translated many times, and it presents a roadmap for living a life of peace and joy, for example, with the eventual end point being complete balance and happiness with your life. In Verse 25, Lao Tzu is discussing his views on the origins of the universe. He describes the energy that created the universe as the Tao, which, based on my Christian upbringing and my interpretation of this verse, means God to me. It then goes on to use the word great to describe heaven, the earth and all of its people, which means that everything, including you and me are a part of this perfect, formless energy that resides within us. The word great is used several times within the body of the verse and the last line of the verse uses the word great as a call to action by simply stating "understand the great within yourself."

Not only does verse 25 help you to understand that you already have greatness within you, it asks you to accept that there is greatness within everyone and every thing. Reading that verse helped me to experience the biggest *AHA* moment of my life. I realized that I am a part of the very same greatness that created the earth, the trees, the oceans and all people. And so are you! When you begin to think of yourself in this way, you understand that just because you are here right now, your life has a purpose and that you bring your unique gifts to share just by being yourself. Your value isn't determined by external factors, such as how you're viewed by others, what you look like, what your station is in life or whether or not you're accepted by anyone. This greatness that is already within you is yours simply because you're here and are alive and breathing right now. This same greatness also has the ability to do exceptional things in service to the world, and comprehending that concept about yourself levels the playing field between you and everyone else. It's almost impossible for you not to think of yourself as being a part of a larger plan, which opens the door for you to extend kindness toward yourself and others.

I encourage you to get your own copy of the Tao Te Ching so that you can experience the wisdom within those 82 verses for yourself.

Once you embrace these concepts and understand them, the way that you respond to people changes for the better. Most notably, you'll begin to see yourself in every person that you encounter, which will soften the way that you treat them. You'll develop an attitude of respect, accepting others for all of their idiosyncrasies, even those you might be conditioned to label as faults. It is through this acceptance that the door opens for kindness to come through.

It can be easy to see kindness as reciprocal, only extending it when someone offers you a kindness first. But once you make a habit of offering it frequently and without condition, you begin to reap the rewards of it for yourself in how you feel. Remember your greatness always, so that you can experience the rewards that being truly kind offers you.

Focus on how kindness feels

I wanted to experience for myself what it feels like to offer kindness regularly, so I began a little private experiment. There is a Starbucks that is not too far from my home, and I sometimes pass by it when I'm running errands. On a few occasions, I have gone through their drive through and arranged to pay for the coffee of the person behind me as well as my own. This is a small act, but its effect is big. It felt good to pay for someone else's coffee. I didn't want any accolades or to even be noticed for it. I simply wanted to do it with no thanks required.

On another occasion, I witnessed a gentleman in the parking lot of my local grocery store having a bad day. He was standing next to his car, visibly upset and reduced to tears, so I approached him and asked if everything was OK and whether there was anything that I could do for him. Through his sobs, he told me that he was having a bad day and had just received some terrible news, but he thanked me for asking. I continued to talk to him while he pulled himself together. Once he was on his way, I continued with my day, feeling pretty good about helping a stranger, even if what I offered didn't seem like much. You just never know how much an offering of kindness, no matter what it is, can be of value to someone else.

You also have to be willing to accept kindness. Many of us don't know what to do when someone directs a kindness our way. We have lost the ability to not only offer but to even accept a simple kindness from one another. We are so wrapped up in our thoughts that we can't focus on all of the good things that are happening all around us. Instead, we remain laser-focused on the constant stream of thinking that tells us that we don't measure up. Self-doubt diverts our attention away from all of the goodness that is right in front of us. It doesn't have to be this way. You know by now that you have greatness inside of you and you also already understand that any negative thought that you have about yourself is just your ego talking. So, tell your ego to knock it off by choosing a different thought at the exact moment that you experience a negative one. Purposefully stop and redirect your thoughts to something that you know is great about yourself and you'll instantly see the world around you and your thoughts change for the better.

It sounds difficult, but I promise that it gets easier the more you practice. There is a freedom that you gain by being in control of your ego. By telling your ego to knock it off, you become free from all of the untrue negative ruminations about yourself that you experience in your mind, and it's this freedom that tells these thoughts that they no longer have a place to hang out with you. They will no longer have an influence over how you view your life, and more importantly, how you view your present. Almost immediately, you will notice that your self-esteem and your confidence levels increase.

Ways to be kind

Always keep kindness in the front of your mind. Specifically, remain aware of how you can be kind to everyone that comes across your path each day. You don't need a reason to do it, being kind can be the reason in and of itself. Every person you meet is going through something, even though it may not be apparent what they are dealing with on the inside. An act of kindness can go a long way into making their day great and also in making you feel good, too.

Her are a few possibilities to get you to think about how you can act on being kind to others. Give it a look and feel free to use some or all of these suggestions for yourself.

- Give a stranger a smile.
- Lend an ear when someone needs to talk and remain fully present with them.
- Act in thoughtful ways without expecting anything in return.
- Eradicate judgement toward others from your thoughts.
- Be kind to yourself by doing something every day that makes you feel fulfilled.
- Hold a door open for someone.
- Simply ask someone how they're doing when you see them. And then really listen.

Kindness is contagious, and even the smallest act of kindness can have a compounding effect on society. When you do something kind for someone else, that energy gets sent out into the world in waves and contributes positively to changing the social fabric around us. Being kind will also contribute to how connected you feel to other people and will add significant meaning and fun to your life. Kindness is its own reward!

Five actions to activate your kindness

- *Remember your greatness. Anytime that you're feeling "less than," remind yourself that you come from something great and that you also have this same greatness within you. Your confidence and self-esteem will increase and when you feel better about yourself, it's even easier to be kind.*

- *Become more observant of people around you and tap into your compassion when you see someone who is struggling. Then use the compassion that you feel to offer them a kindness. They won't feel alone and it will give them a boost, which just may spur them to offer a kindness to someone else.*

- *Carve out a few hours of your time each month to volunteer. Tutor children or volunteer with a nonprofit in your city that can use your skills and expertise, for example. The time that you give each month will remind you to always keep kindness front and center in your thoughts and actions.*

- *Always say please and thank you for everything, but when you express it, really feel your gratitude. This conscious act serves as a constant reminder to keep kindness front and center in your thoughts.*
- *Assume positive intent in all of your interactions. When someone does or says something that rubs you the wrong way, try to understand what their position is first before settling on a conclusion. This will prevent you from responding in an unkind way and give you a chance to clear the air before a situation escalates.*

No act of kindness is too small, and acting in a kind way has the potential to spread exponentially through the world. Keep this famous quote from the famous novelist Henry James in your mind: "Three things in human life are important: the first is to be kind, the second is to be kind. And the third is to be kind."

CHAPTER 9

Activate Humility and Gain Perspective

Our discussion of kindness feeds well into the importance of having humility. There really is a special bond between kindness and humility. Kind people have great relationships with themselves, which gives them the ability to easily relate to other people. Being able to relate to others is one of the keys to humility.

My late grandfather was a great example of someone who lived with humility. He was a very kind man and could have a conversation with anyone, no matter who they were or what their station was in life, and he could walk away from any conversation with a perfect stranger having made a new friend. His ability to relate to others was an example of just how humble he really was. He didn't grow up with much, and this helped to shape his view on how he interacted with other people. He refused to see any differences between himself and anyone else. As a result, he had many connections that he could call on at any time if he needed help. These relationships added meaning to his life and gave him perspective on how important human relationships are to our survival.

We're living in a time where practicing humility doesn't seem to carry any importance. You see examples of this on social media, where people alternate between being boastful and tearing each other down, and are quick to be cruel and insensitive. Treating each other with respect is a lost art while those that are the loudest and seek validation by espousing how great they believe themselves to be are rewarded for their efforts with hollow accolades and praise.

While acting in these ego driven ways may pay off in the short run, there is a long-term detriment to not having activated humility. We'll discuss those as we get further into the chapter, but for now, I'd like to share with you my personal journey to discovering my own humility.

How I learned about humility

When I was younger, I didn't have a lot of confidence in myself and was easily influenced by the thoughts and opinions of other people. This naiveté ended up being a real detriment to my growth because it caused me to hold on to false ideas and opinions, especially in my perceptions of other people. This quickly became clear to me when I left home to go to college.

I went to school in a large metropolitan area, a melting pot of different cultures and progressive ideas. I was excited about developing new friendships and getting to know new people, but that excitement had unspoken strings attached to it— the people that I wanted to meet had to be just like me. Now, I didn't grow up in a household that put this idea in my mind. Nobody taught me that if someone was different, that they were flawed or lacked respect. The message from my parents was the exact opposite, in fact, but I had still developed negative opinions about cultures and people that didn't match that narrative that was firmly in place in my mind. I was closed off and rigid, and while I didn't express my negative views outwardly, I certainly did think them.

All of this changed at the beginning of the first semester of my sophomore year. On the first day of classes, I was sitting in a class, waiting for the professor to arrive, when a guy that was at the desk beside of me struck up a conversation. He told me that he was from India and we began to swap stories with one another about how we ended up at this particular university. He explained how he was nervous about being there because he didn't know anyone and that the size of the school really intimidated him. At first, I kept him at arms-length, but over time, I began to let my guard down and our friendship with one another began to grow. My view of him shifted in a way that helped me to see how much we had in common. As time went on, he began to introduce me to several of his new friends, who were also from different cultures, and I returned the favor. All of us frequently had lunch at the student union together and we studied for our exams together. We remained friends throughout the rest of our time in school, but after we graduated and moved into working full time, we slowly lost touch with one another.

I don't know where he is today, but I am so grateful for the influence that he had on my views. He didn't realize it, but he taught me how to embrace and accept other people for who they are, and he unknowingly helped me to get over my fear of the differences that I perceived in other people. I realized that deep down inside, all of us are the same and that all of us want the same things in life. Despite appearances, differences in religion and language, and so on, we all have unique gifts and experiences that we can offer to one another. The lessons that I learned were very humbling and they were also the catalyst to change my views. I realized that my arrogance toward others, muted though it was, and my unwillingness to welcome different ideas and people into my life were getting in the way of experiences that could enrich and enhance my growth. Acknowledging that reality helped me to move past those long held and unfounded beliefs. As a result, I find myself today continuing my growth and understanding by seeking out people of different cultures, races, ideas and religions so that I can understand their lives and what they offer to the world. Rewarding friendships have developed as a result of my humility and my world view has changed positively.

Humble people express a willingness to learn new and sometimes uncomfortable things and they also build trust and mutual respect with those that they interact with. Some of the most effective leaders have high levels of humility that began with their first being honest with themselves about their shortcomings and then making efforts to overcome them. Their willingness to accept advice from and work hand in hand with people who don't hold the same beliefs help them to experience success.

When you develop an accurate picture of yourself, including both what you have to offer as well as your limitations, opening yourself up to changing yourself for the better, you become an example of humility.

The habits of humble people

When I was still working in corporate America, I was having a discussion with the Senior Director of the group that I worked in about upcoming metrics development for the following year. During our conversation, he stopped midstream and said something to me about one of my leadership peers. He said that she was a bit too passive and insecure and that she placated her team too much. He viewed her as weak and wanted her out, replaced by someone with a "stronger presence." I was immediately taken aback because this wasn't my experience with her at all, and I was uncomfortable with him gossiping about her. To me, she seemed knowledgeable and thoughtful, and most importantly, she was a great leader who was always open to hearing new ideas. Her team loved her because of her recognition of their efforts and how she expressed her gratitude for them, and they bent over backwards to help her accomplish her goals.

My trust for this Senior Director evaporated immediately. This peer of mine was incredibly confident and she had plenty of competency in executing the duties of her job. She knew what needed to be done and she produced solid, dependable results. She was respected even more by her peers because she didn't trumpet her accomplishments and boast about herself. Instead, she spoke frequently about the good things that her team was doing and talked about them in a positive, supportive way. Though I never discussed the Senior Director's thoughts with her, one day she told me that she was fully aware of how she was viewed by certain members of leadership, but she was adamant that she wasn't going to let that stop her from continuing to produce great results for the company. She continued on, unfazed, and did a great job.

I share this with you because I want you to see what the personification of humility looks like. People with humility build and retain strong relationships with others, they don't boast about their accomplishments, they put other people ahead of themselves, are active listeners, they face challenges with poise and grace and they frequently express how grateful they are. They listen to feedback, make any necessary adjustments, and ask for help when they need it.

No matter what your role is in life, having humility is one of the keys to your overall happiness and success. Everyone that you come in contact with every day is trying to accomplish the same thing that you are, which is to successfully move through their life. While the things that they're trying to accomplish may not look exactly like what you're trying to accomplish, they're doing so in the best way that they know how. Having humility helps you to understand and accept this as well as the differences that you perceive.

The advantages of activated humility

It's natural to feel like you're invisible when you notice that society rewards the overconfident and narcissistic, but don't buy into that worldview. Being narcissistic and overconfident is an "on the surface" behavior that requires consistent "on the surface" responses from other people to keep it alive. It's difficult, maybe even impossible, to develop real connections that have meaning and depth from interactions like these. People who have activated humility already know this, and they purposefully choose to draw little or no attention to themselves. They stay under the radar, and the quality of the connections that they have is stronger and longer lasting, which aids in contributing to feeling fulfilled. My humble colleague is a real testament to the good that can happen for someone who is humble. She went on to experience significant growth in her career, moving into a challenging and satisfying role with an international company that values her experience and dependable results. She was able to move into this new role because her humility, work ethic and professionalism were remembered by a previous colleague who hired her to help support his team.

Humility also helps you to learn and grow. This is because you are open to new ways of viewing things and are curious about the possibilities that life can offer you. It's impossible to learn if you think of yourself as already knowing everything. Every day brings new opportunities to learn and to grow, and people who are humble understand this and purposefully seek out these opportunities.

With humility also comes self-awareness. Some believe that people who are humble have a low opinion of themselves and that they also lack confidence, which couldn't be further from the truth. Instead, when you're humble, you know exactly what your talents are and you also know your limitations. You then use these talents to the benefit of yourself and others and spend time working on the areas that you know need to be improved. As a result, humble people tend to experience more success in their life.

There's also real freedom in humility. When you're humble, you don't feel like you need to live your life measuring it against someone else's yardstick. You have a strong inner compass that you trust and which also helps you to successfully navigate life's challenges with ease and comfort. Your sense of well-being is enhanced, and the subsequent confidence that comes with that helps you to attract the right people into your life. By activating humility into your life, I promise you that you will notice many advantages that will lead to increased meaning and connection.

The traps of activated humility

Unlike many of the values we have discussed, there are times when being humble can be a hindrance to your success. Luckily, there are solutions for this. Let's take a look at some of the possible traps that you may face from being humble.

The first thing you may notice is that people underestimate your abilities. This was the case with my former co-worker, and she naturally overcame this obstacle by consistently speaking up and sharing her ideas on how we could tackle a challenge that all of us shared with one another. She was viewed as being a trusted subject matter expert and held prominence on the team, despite her humble approach.

You may also notice that people view you as being a follower rather than a leader, never standing up for what you believe in. Again, combat this by freely sharing your insights or thoughts on the topic at hand. Never shrink down from thoughtfully offering up your ideas or suggestions because you're afraid of them being shot down or ridiculed. No-one is going to agree with you 100% of the time, but you will be respected for having the tenacity to stand by your beliefs.

People may also believe that they can take advantage of you. Tap into your already activated courage and kindness to put a stop to this. It will feel uncomfortable, and you may also be fearful at first, but summon the courage to set boundaries and limits to what you are willing to accept or put up with from other people and then stand firmly by them without exception. You will be respected by others, and more importantly, you will have a high level of self-respect.

You may feel like you're viewed as being weak. Keep in mind that when you are humble, you don't let your pride run your life, so other's opinions of you don't even register. You also don't think that you are any more clever or are smarter than anyone else. Thoughts of competition don't enter your mind, which can be difficult to deal with, given the high level of competition that is in our society today. There's great strength in knowing what you're good at and what your limitations are, and then using that knowledge to your benefit.

Five suggestions to activate your humility

- *Consciously look for ways to be of service to others every day. We discussed this concept in chapter 2 and it applies to activated humility, as well. Be of service by letting someone in front of you in line or hold a door open for someone, for example. Doing so puts you in the mindset of focusing on the needs of others instead of yourself.*

- *Do not pass judgment about how you believe other people should be behaving. Always assume positive intent when you're evaluating other people's actions.*

By doing this, you gain clarity on why they might be doing something in the way that they are, and this helps to positively shape your response to them.

- *Employ your active listening skills and talk less. Stay present and engaged in a conversation and ask questions. This makes the person talking feel good about themselves and shows that you care about what they think.*

- *Appreciate what other people do for you. This carries a lot of influence because it shows others that you value and care about them.*

- *Appreciate and celebrate the individual talents of everyone. Because we're human, we have limitations and none of us can do everything. Recognize that the talents that each of us individually offer to the world are small pieces in a giant puzzle that ultimately serves to benefit each of us.*

When you live a life of activated humility, you gain a new perspective over the critical areas of your life. You begin to witness a renewed sense of inner strength and confidence that may have been absent previously, your interactions with other people become more positive because of the new way that you look at them individually and you get a renewed sense of your place in the world and how you fit into it. The outlook that you hold about your future brightens and you gain full command over your actions toward other people.

CHAPTER 10

Activate Forgiveness and Put the Past Behind You

I n 1711, Alexander Pope wrote in his *An Essay on Criticism* that "to err is human, to forgive divine." While the first part of the quote, "to err is human," is widely known, the second part "to forgive divine" tends to be forgotten. It stands out to me not only because within those seven words, there is a lot of wisdom for living a peaceful and contented life.

The act of forgiveness is something that everyone struggles with sometimes. It's difficult to let go of perceived and real offenses that you will most assuredly experience and it's even more difficult to let go of the subsequent anger, resentment and grudges that come as a result of these experiences. Again, the ego always thinks it's correct, and it wants to keep you wrapped up in past events, which has a detrimental impact on your present.

It doesn't have to be this way. You can learn to activate forgiveness and use it as an eraser to wipe away any anger or resentment that you hold in your heart. This frees you to be more present and available to other people and changes your mindset to be more optimistic as you go through the remaining experiences of your life.

How forgiveness feels

You likely already have an understanding of what forgiveness is, so rather than spending time focusing on its definition, let's concentrate more on the feelings that you can expect to experience from practicing it

When someone has wronged you in the past, you probably felt really bad, with your mind churning through thoughts, asking yourself *how could they do that?* or *who do they think they are?* Sound familiar? If you haven't fully forgiven that person by now, those thoughts might still have a hold on you today. Maybe you still feel anger, resentment or revenge when they pop back into your consciousness. These feelings keep you shackled to an event that has probably long been forgotten by the offender. What's more, those feelings act as a weight on your interactions and connections to other people that are in your life right now. If you want to be truly free emotionally, you have to extend forgiveness.

My own experience with offering forgiveness is complicated and messy. It took a long time to activate it in my own circumstances, and I was well into my forties before I finally figured out that I was still holding on to grudges and hurt feelings from events that occurred over twenty years before. Some of the events that I remained attached to were from things that happened all the way back to my childhood. These memories would pop up when I was in my car driving somewhere and my mind drifted off, while I was working around the house and some were even triggered in conversations with people who inadvertently reminded me of some past offense. I would notice an instant negative change in my mood and then those old feelings of resentment and anger would surface again. I could feel my stomach twist up and I would mentally check out of the conversation because my focus had turned toward those negative feelings. Eventually, I would bring myself back to the present, only to return to experiencing the same feelings again when I was alone.

It is detrimental to hold on to unforgiven past offense because doing so keeps you from finding meaning and connection in the present moment. Refusing to forgive locks you into an emotional prison in your mind, but it becomes easier to break free of that prison when you bring activated forgiveness into your life. As with pretty much anything that you do, the more you practice forgiveness, the easier it gets and you will notice that it yields more positive results for you as you focus on the good feelings that you experience from it.

It takes a lot of your emotional energy to carry the burden of past events around in your mind. It affects how you feel mentally and physically every day, which has an effect on your level of happiness. When you forgive, you free yourself from the burden of carrying thoughts that sap you of your precious energy. Have you ever noticed how you feel worn down and a little cloudy mentally when you have been thinking about something for extended periods of time? Well, holding grudges works the same way. When you think about the large amounts of time that you have spent ruminating over an unforgivable event in your mind, you realize pretty quickly that the energy spent on that could have been used toward something more productive. It's freeing to forgive and let go, and when you feel free, you're happy, you're lighter and your mood is better. When you put your past behind you through forgiveness, your energy level increases, freeing you to focus on the things that interest you or make you feel satisfied and help in your personal growth.

Forgiveness is only for you

To your ego, forgiveness sounds like you're giving a pass to someone that may have hurt you in some way. But remember that your ego makes you believe false narratives about yourself and other people. The truth is that forgiveness is all about you and is only for you. When you forgive, you aren't saying that what someone else did to you is OK. What you are saying is that you are willing to move past your hurt so that you don't spend time thinking about it. Spending your time ruminating on such things builds anger and resentment, and these emotions easily take up residence in your mind.

Forgiving someone is a one-person job. You don't have to make a big show of it and call or write the person who hurt you to tell them that you've forgiven them. They don't even need to know that they are forgiven. It's also not something that is going to come at the snap of a finger, either. Forgiveness is a process that you have to go through so that you come out better on the other side of it. It's not easy and it takes time, but is well worth the effort.

The first thing to do is to is to take some time for introspection and to look for the silver lining of what happened. When I started doing this, I realized that I learned several lessons about how not to treat other people. In this respect, the person or persons who hurt me in the past were some of the greatest teachers that I've ever had, helping me shape my actions in a way that prevented me from causing pain to someone else. Another part of the process is to look at the person who hurt you with some compassion and empathy, which can be quite challenging. When you look at someone from this perspective, you see that they, just like you, are also trying to make their way in the world the best way that they know how. Understanding this helps you to see their human side and makes it easier to begin forgiving them. Another part of the process is to always be mindful of having peaceful thoughts in your mind toward your offender. I'm a big believer in karma, and while you may never see them learn their own lessons for their past choices, have peace by knowing that their lesson will come for them in some form. When you make adopting and relaying peaceful thoughts toward your offender a part of your forgiveness, you become peaceful yourself on the inside. This peace is then radiated out to the people that you come in contact with every day and helps you to establish strong connections with them.

Forgiveness does not mean that you have to reconcile with the person who hurt you. It also doesn't mean that have to pick up where you left off and continue merrily on your way with them. Only you can decide how you want to proceed in a relationship that has been damaged by hurt. Tell the other person how they made you feel and gauge their reaction. If they are understanding and humble and you feel like you want to give it another go, tread lightly, but go into it with a positive mindset so that you don't inadvertently sabotage the relationship before giving it a chance. If you begin to notice the same behaviors occurring again, then you'll have to reevaluate what you want to do, and if it means cutting ties, then do so. Your energy is too precious to waste on those who can't or won't treat you with respect and dignity.

Forgive Yourself

It can be much easier to forgive someone else than to forgive yourself. I struggled with self-forgiveness for a good period of my life, and it manifested itself with sleepless nights where I tossed and turned and let my thoughts run out of control. The next day, the negative feelings around what I did were amplified because I was exhausted. For your own emotional well-being and so that you can move beyond the situation, you have to learn how to forgive your own mistakes that you've made.

When you forgive yourself, you're not telling yourself that what you did to someone else was OK, you're developing an understanding of what happened and are willing to move past it without letting your guilty or angry thoughts at yourself take over your life. Compassion for yourself is the main focus, because without it, it will be difficult to move on. Give yourself a break and accept that you're a human being and are prone to mistakes and then use the following guidance to put the event behind you.

Start by owning up to the actions that you took that hurt someone else. Take some time to review what happened and why so that you don't find yourself in the same situation again. Try to put yourself in the recipient's shoes and understand how they must have felt. It will be a little painful, but with that pain comes growth, and if you can get past this point of taking responsibility for your actions, you're well on your way to forgiving yourself.

Let yourself experience the guilt that you're feeling. It's uncomfortable but that's actually a good thing because it will serve as a reminder to redirect your behavior in a positive direction the next time. Don't get mired down in guilt - if you've hurt someone, it doesn't necessarily mean that you're a bad person, it just means that you made a choice that had a bad outcome.

Tell the person that you've hurt that you're sorry, and really mean it, and then let yourself off the hook. Apologizing may not get you the result that you expect, and that's OK, but what it does give you is the knowledge that you did everything that you could. That can provide a lot of restful nights of sleep and a clear conscience going forward.

None of this is meant to give you a pass to continue hurting others with your bad choices. The idea behind self-forgiveness is that you learn from your experience so that you can continue to progress in your life. Understand why you did what you did and how you can prevent yourself from making the same mistake again. With your learning comes a new and better way to treat and understand others, which can only enhance your connection with them.

How forgiveness benefits you

When I was struggling with forgiveness, my ego loved to take over my thoughts and tell me that I shouldn't forgive and that the other person didn't deserve any of my time and effort. I thought that it would be much easier to hold a grudge for a while, hoping that the passage of time would wipe everything away. Unfortunately, you just can't sweep not forgiving under the rug and expect everything to be good. Grudges turn to resentment, which leads to an overall drop in happiness, and then your interactions with other people go south. This makes practicing forgiveness an imperative, and you can expect to receive many good things in return for your efforts.

One of the first things that you'll notice is that when you forgive, you're happier. Forgiving calms your ego down and makes you feel at peace inside, which then lets good thoughts flow freely in your mind. You're no longer tangled up in your hurt, feeling stuck and frustrated. You are free to enjoy your relationships with other people.

Forgiveness also helps you keep relationships alive. It's inevitable that a friend or loved one will say or do something that hurts or disappoints you at some point, and when you don't forgive them, you eventually lose your trust in them. Your willingness to compromise or cooperate goes out the window and eventually destroys the relationship that you've built. Forgiveness repairs the wounds and stabilizes the relationship.

Forgiveness also makes you kinder. We already know that being kind can help you connect with others, and it also boosts feelings of generosity. People who forgive are more likely to volunteer in their community or donate to a charity and their kindness adds meaning to their life because they're spending their time with people who think like they do and giving to organizations that support their beliefs.

Forgiveness can also improve your health. When you're dealing with the stress of holding grudges or being angry and resentful, your blood pressure and your heart rate can go up. With stress comes increases in cortisol in your system, which contributes to inflammation. When you practice forgiveness, your blood pressure drops and your immune system gets a boost, which helps you to fight off illness.

The foundation for forgiving others and yourself lie in compassion, empathy and understanding. Use this foundation for yourself so that you can put the past behind you and have a life full of meaning and connection.

A final thought....

I once read a quote by Dr. Wayne Dyer that said "if you're looking for an occasion to be offended, you're going to find it." When someone hurts you, it goes without question that the feelings that you experience are very real to you. Before you make a judgement about the situation, take some time to take a step back and carefully evaluate what is happening to you in the moment that you believe that someone has hurt you. All of us have our triggers, and something that might make you feel hurt might have no effect on someone else whatsoever and vice versa. While I'm not trying to downplay what you may be experiencing, try not to spend your time seeking out ways to find fault in what someone else has done.

It's very easy to let our petty differences and insecurities get in the way of maintaining fulfilling relationships with people that we like or love. You're the one that's in the driver's seat when it comes to how you react, so the next time that you experience a hurt or an offense that you believe has been directed your way, take a step back so that you can calmly assess what has happened. When you give yourself a little breathing room, you get an opportunity to understand the context of the event and can make a determination on its effect on you with a clear head. If you still feel hurt, follow the steps that we've already talked about to work through your forgiveness, but by all means forgive them.

Five suggestions to activate your forgiveness

- *Make a list of the people who you believe have hurt you and then meditate on offering them forgiveness. This frees you to no longer carry around any anger, resentment or bitterness that you may be holding in your mind.*

- *Forgive yourself. Make a list of the people that you may have hurt in the past, reflect on why you hurt them and then reach out to them, if you are able, and ask for their forgiveness. If the relationship is salvageable, it establishes goodwill with the person that you have hurt and helps to maintain and strengthen the connection that you have with one another.*

- *To keep your forgiveness top of mind, periodically go back and review the list of people that you believe that you have hurt in the past. This can be painful, but its purpose is to remind you how not to treat others going forward so that having to ask for forgiveness becomes less frequent.*
- *Remind yourself that you have total control over your reactions. You can control how you respond to people and situations and you can carefully and objectively evaluate how you perceive you're being treated.*
- *Take your focus off of how you're feeling. Consistently thinking about how someone else has hurt you turns all of your power over to them. When you stop focusing on your feelings, you get the breathing space that you need to clear your mind and to evaluate the situation with a clear mind. You may just discover that there was nothing to forgive and naturally move on.*

Without forgiveness, you stay locked in your past and it becomes difficult to let go and allow a better future to arrive for you. No one is perfect, so practice letting yourself and others off the hook for making mistakes. You'll free yourself from living in the past and pave the way for new and fulfilling present and future moments.

Conclusion

I n the introduction to this book, I mentioned how a common traffic event inspired me to begin reflecting on the sub-optimal state of human interactions today. I also mentioned that I believe that modern day demands and the fast pace of life have moved society away from focusing on the human values that bind us to one another. After reading this book, I hope that these difficulties will no longer be a challenge for you.

No matter what twists and turns life may throw your way, you are always in charge of how you respond to any situation. By activating the values we've talked about, you will find yourself to always be in charge of your reactions to other people and situations that you encounter going forward because of your new found way thinking about yourself, other people and external events.

You've learned how activated compassion begins by first extending compassion to yourself, so that you are better able to discern when someone else may need it from you. You've also learned how putting too much emphasis on what other people think of you can affect how you feel about yourself, which then affects your ability to offer your love to others. You've learned how being humble can give you a renewed sense of inner strength and confidence, and you've learned how activating forgiveness can help you put the past behind you and make you feel happier right now.

The ten human values discussed in this book highlight your path and your mission going forward so that you can experience lasting meaning and connection in your life. It's my hope that when you activate them for yourself that you feel a brand-new beginning for you and any relationship that you have, now or in the future. Every chapter of this book has prepared you for the goodness that is about to come your way.

Now that you have all of the tools that you need to establish a fulfilling life brought to you through increased meaning and connection, go forward and live your humanity.

Acknowledgments

The ideas in this book are the result of the many teachable moments that occurred throughout my life. Little did I know that they would become the best experiences that I could ever have, paving the way for living my own humanity.

I received countless amounts of generous support while writing this book, and for that I am eternally grateful. The well wishes, encouragement and inquiries on the book's progress provided the occasional push to turn an idea into a physical reality.

I want to thank William Boggess, who provided excellent editing guidance and who also shared his expertise to help steer this first-time author on to the best writing path. I also want to thank all of the folks at Morgan James Publishing, specifically David Hancock, Jim Howard and Stephanie McLawhorn, for taking me under their wings and helping to get my ideas into the world.

About the Author

A fter a 25-year career in Corporate Finance, Ron Hammond is now focusing his efforts on examining how our thoughts about ourselves and others affect our connections. Born and raised in Virginia, Ron now lives in Denver, CO where he holds a private pilot license and enjoys skiing, biking and reading in his free time.

A free ebook edition is available with the purchase of this book.

To claim your free ebook edition:

1. Visit MorganJamesBOGO.com
2. Sign your name CLEARLY in the space
3. Complete the form and submit a photo of the entire copyright page
4. You or your friend can download the ebook to your preferred device

A **FREE** ebook edition is available for you or a friend with the purchase of this print book.

CLEARLY SIGN YOUR NAME ABOVE

Instructions to claim your free ebook edition:
1. Visit MorganJamesBOGO.com
2. Sign your name CLEARLY in the space above
3. Complete the form and submit a photo of this entire page
4. You or your friend can download the ebook to your preferred device

Print & Digital Together Forever.

Snap a photo

Free ebook

Read anywhere